7 Steps to Joyful Living

The User Manual for Human Life

Suresh Kumar K.K

Copyright © 2025 by Suresh Kumar K.K

All rights reserved.

This book or any portion thereof may not be reproduced or used in any manner whatsoever without the express written permission of the respective author of the respective story, except for the use of brief quotations in a book review.

The writer of the respective work holds sole responsibility for the originality of the content and IndiePress is not responsible in any way whatsoever.

Printed in India

IndiePress

ISBN: 978-93-7197-097-6

Second Edition 2025, First Edition 2023.

IndiePress

A division of Nasadiya Technologies Private Ltd.

Koramangala, Bengaluru

Karnataka-560029

http://indiepress.in/

Book Cover designed by Prahlad Gopakumar & Subin Shyam

Dedicated to Anand, Preethi, and their children, whose pain and agony deeply moved me, inspiring me to write this book for the benefit of many.

My Sincere Gratitude To

My mother, father, and sisters, who have been pillars of love, care, sacrifice, and support since the beginning of my life, helped me pursue my dreams.

My wife, daughter, and son, who have tirelessly contributed to making our home a place of love and care, supporting my dreams and understanding my absence when I was busy pursuing them.

My grandparents, parents' siblings, their spouses and children, my in-laws, and their families have always prioritised love and affection, celebrating every joyous occasion and mourning every loss together as one big family.

All my teachers who patiently guided me, from my first alphabet lessons at the age of four to everything I know today, and the spiritual gurus who guided me in gaining a deeper understanding of life.

Doctors, healers, psychologists, researchers, scientists, trainers, coaches, and many others—including my friends—have contributed to my life and shared their wisdom on the topics explored in this book.

I am deeply humbled and blessed by the contributions of others to my journey and endeavours, without which it would not have been possible to present this book to you in its current form.

Contents

Preface 1

The Pain of a Human Being 6

    The Most Important Job 11

Step 1: Discover Yourself 15

    Your Birth and You.. 20

        The Scientific View 24

        Karma Philosophy... 25

        The Real You 31

    Demystifying Success.. 34

    Love What You Do 39

    Needs and Desires 40

Step 2: Master Your Mind... 49

    How the Mind Works 50

    Training Your Mind 55

    Mindfulness... 62

    Meditation 65

        Observing Thoughts 67

        Observing Body Sensations 70

    Healthy Mind 71

Step 3: Health First 73
    Diseases 76
    Physical Fitness 78
    Breath 83
    Food 85
        Vegetarian vs Non-Vegetarian 90
        Fasting 92
    Sleep 94
    Self-Care 95
    A Healthy Body 100

Step 4: Love and Relationships 103
    Love 104
    Relationships 107
    Marriage 112
        Choosing a Partner 114
        Commitment 117
        Extramarital Relationships 120
        Conflicts 123
    Your Options 129

Step 5: Righteousness 133
    Your Biggest Ally 140

Step 6: Excellence 145
Education 147
Four Types of Work 152
Path of Excellence 155
Teamwork 163
Workplace Culture 167
Three Types of People 169
The Art of Saying 'No' 171
Effective Communication 172
Fear and Failure 174
Retirement 186

Step 7: Gratitude 191

Death 195
Regrets in Life 197
Dying Early 201
Death and Beyond 205
Science 206
Karma 207

Celebrate Your Life 210

Preface

Understanding yourself, knowing what is best for you, doing that with absolute involvement, and being happy and joyful may not come naturally to even 10 percent of the human population.

Surprising, isn't it?

Human life has the highest potential and possibility compared to any other life on the planet. However, human beings are also the ones grappling with the basics of life, diminishing its spirit and beauty.

What a paradox.

They struggle to understand themselves, manage their thoughts and emotions, stay physically fit, pursue education that aligns with their passions, build strong relationships, navigate marriage and parenting, excel at work, cope with failure and setbacks, and find meaning in life.

You need a holistic approach to life to fix all of them and to succeed, by blending theory to gain knowledge with practice to implement change.

This book is exactly about that.

This book takes you through simple steps to understand your composition, conditioning, strengths, needs, desires, possibilities, and responsibilities—helping you discover yourself, train your body and mind, unlock your potential, navigate challenges at home and work, and truly celebrate life.

It covers everything from your birth to death, and the life in between, as a user manual for your life.

Since childhood, witnessing human suffering has caused me the most pain. Regardless of age, gender, wealth, social status, knowledge, experience, place of living, or circumstances, human beings continue to suffer, much of it being self-inflicted.

In my quest to understand and alleviate this suffering, I pursued extensive formal education and gained experience across various fields—including research, product development, and business development—creating many award-winning products and businesses.

I also founded 'eseLife', a venture dedicated to offering products and services to make life easier and happier for everyone.

I have learned and meticulously practiced Yoga and various types of meditation taught by spiritual gurus and practitioners. I have studied the essence of the Mahabharata, Ramayana, Bhagavad Gita, Bible, Quran, and many other epics and scriptures. My travels took me around the world, often alone, and extensively through the Himalayas in search of truth.

Countless interactions with researchers, psychologists, doctors, neuroscientists, pranic and Reiki healers, parapsychology practitioners, and spiritual leaders have been invaluable in this journey.

Preface

My passion and practice in martial arts, rifle shooting, swimming, squash, marathon running, vegetable gardening, acting in the theatre and films, creative and product design, and community service have all helped me broaden my perspectives and enabled me to write this book based on my life experiences and what has worked for me, as well as for a wider audience who have sought my guidance.

I have spent considerable time supporting others to expand and explore possibilities to lead a life they are proud of. I often missed meals, sleep, and time with family and friends in that endeavour, but my love and concern for every human being motivated me to continue it to this day, as a responsibility greater than my own needs and comfort for the well-being of many.

It is the same motivation that has helped me to write this book and bring it to you for your benefit. Of course, the experience and learning from it helped me become a better version of myself.

This book is not merely for reading and enjoyment but for internalising, practising, and living by its concepts. I have kept the content simple, real, and authentic. I summoned the energy and courage to do so for your benefit.

It may upset your illusions and strip away your pretensions. If you are willing to listen, postpone your judgement, reconsider your beliefs, explore possibilities, integrate reality, and transform your life for the better, then you have the right guide here.

The reader reviews have been highly encouraging and most note the book's uniqueness as follows:

- A comprehensive, theory-oriented, practical approach with step-by-step guidance to achieve success, happiness, and joy.

- Profound ideas are simplified through storytelling and relatable anecdotes, allowing a wide range of readers to relate, absorb, reflect, and implement change.

- Sincere, intimate, and friendly, covering all the aspects of human existence and happiness as a genuine guide for personal growth, in an engaging and gripping narrative.

- Not offering advice but resembling a heartfelt, friendly chat with a wise friend, inviting readers to reflect on their own lives and choices and subtly motivating them to take action.

Additionally, I host a 'Joyful Living' workshop designed for individuals from all walks of life to delve deeper into the seven steps outlined in this book and enrich their understanding through experiential learning.

Here, let me share a cross-section of the feedback from hundreds of participants from multiple workshops over the years.

'Wonderful sessions, connecting the dots, and well-articulated. One of a kind and one of the best learning experiences in my life.' - **Business Head**

'It helped me to get clarity in my life and career, the importance of collaboration, how to make choices, and love what I do.' - **Working Woman**

'Unique, simple, and very valuable. It will help me in making the right decisions— at work, at home and everywhere—consistently.' – **Bureaucrat**

'It is a relief and a joy for me to understand what is important to me and how to take the necessary steps to become what I truly want to be.'- **Student**

Preface

'Extremely insightful and thought-provoking. I am still immersed in it, and everything around me feels different now. It has had a profound impact on me.' - **Project Manager**

'The exceptional design and organisation of the workshop are truly remarkable. I now have a blueprint for myself. I was unaware of what such a workshop could achieve.' - **Creative Director**

'An amazing experience to understand everything about life in a single day. Simple, practical, and doable formula to do what I am meant to do.' - **Homemaker**

'DNA analysis is amazing. I can think beyond and differently than ever before. It should have been done much earlier. It does not matter; I got it at a critical time.' – **Entrepreneur**

'I have discovered myself and have been deeply moved. I now see everything through a set of different lenses. I am at a loss for words to describe its impact.' – **CEO**

Although I have clearly outlined the 7 Steps, they are not separate but deeply interdependent for your success and happiness. Each step is connected and presented in a specific order to ensure continuity and clarity, so you can better understand, appreciate, and internalise it.

Do not rush through, skip any part, or change the sequence.

Take your time—I will be with you.

I recommend revisiting this book once a year to refresh the concepts and for guidance during challenging times.

Let's begin!

The Pain of a Human Being

Each stage of life demands a different version of you, and it is essential to consciously grow into that role to be successful, happy, and joyful.

Anand hailed from a small town and grew up in a middle-class family with his father, mother, and younger sister. His father worked as an accountant in a private company, while his mother managed the household as a homemaker. He often worked six days a week, rarely took time off, and regularly put in extra hours to supplement the family's income and meet their urgent financial needs.

Anand's mother loved stitching and embroidery and managed to earn a modest income from it. After completing the household chores, she devoted her spare time to sewing, contributing a little extra to the family's finances. To make her work easier and more efficient, Anand's father saved his overtime earnings to buy her a fashion-design sewing machine. With her skills and the new machine, she worked faster and attracted more customers.

Her earnings supported the family during challenging times—whether it was paying for school trips, repairing home appliances, buying a guitar for Anand, or getting new sports shoes for his sister.

They lived in a small rented house, far from the town centre. Although money was limited and resources were scarce, there was no shortage of love, laughter, care, and happiness in the family.

Anand's parents never let their financial difficulties affect their children's education or extracurricular activities. Anand not only played the guitar in a local music band but also excelled in academics, achieving high marks in the engineering entrance examinations. With the help of an education loan, he enrolled in a prestigious college and earned a degree in Biomedical Engineering—although his true aspiration was to become a doctor, motivated by a desire to provide essential medical care to remote villages.

He grew up tall and handsome. His morning runs, evening workouts and disciplined lifestyle made him well built as well. After graduation, he secured a well-paid job at a multinational company, although it wasn't in the field of biomedical equipment he had hoped for. He steadily progressed in his career, repaid his education loan, moved into a new house, bought a car and married a woman called Preethi—all by the age of twenty-eight.

Preethi, a creative designer by profession, first met Anand when she visited his office for an interior design project. Anand noticed her sitting alone in the canteen, enjoying a quiet moment with a cup of coffee. Her elegantly draped saree, the simple, slender necklace, and the soft hairline that gently rose from low on her forehead perfectly matched his image of an ideal woman.

They liked each other from their very first meeting, and it gradually developed into a strong relationship.

I still remember Preethi describing it as, 'like a mosquito bite—we both got infected.' They were willing to sacrifice anything for each other and were married a year later. Since Preethi was from a different town, she resigned from her position and moved to start a new life with Anand.

While their life seemed to be progressing smoothly, Preethi continued to look for job opportunities to resume her career. However, she struggled to find anything in the town that truly aligned with her interests. After two years, they had their daughter. Then, when their daughter turned three, they had a son. With the arrival of their children, Preethi's focus turned to raising them, and she contemplated returning to work once they were older and enrolled in school.

After a couple of years, Anand decided to move into the field of medical devices. In his new position, he worked on developing a low-cost, portable dialysis device that had a significant impact on patients in remote villages. It allowed them to receive treatment in the comfort of their homes, sparing them from spending much of their remaining lives travelling to cities for treatment.

Anand described this as the happiest time of his life, as he was living his dream. I remember him saying that he regularly worked late into the evenings and at weekends, rarely took time off, and didn't even fall ill for a single day during that period, truly enjoying his work.

Once their younger child started school, Preethi eagerly resumed looking for a job, keen to restart her career. After a prolonged search, she finally secured a suitable job—although it was far from their current home and required her to relocate. Anand was progressing well and was happy with his work, so Preethi didn't want to unsettle him and decided to move along with the children, as the job was important for her career restart.

Anand recognised the importance of being there for his family, especially as their children had just started school. He also wanted to support Preethi in her career endeavours. Anand was unable to find a job matching his interests in the new town but secured one at an e-commerce company. Anand made the difficult decision to leave his dream job and the family moved together to the new town.

Moving to an unfamiliar town, change of job for Anand, Preethi working after a long break, and a change of school for the children– all took quite some time to settle down. It was not easy for any of them.

Preethi was often busy taking care of her children's needs, overseeing their studies, balancing her job responsibilities, and attending to household chores, but she never complained. On the other hand, Anand was consumed by meeting quarterly targets, frequently travelling to meet vendors or customers, which left him little time to spend with his family.

Anand found himself unable to make time for important commitments—whether attending parent-teacher meetings at school or visiting his parents, even during medical emergencies, though his sister stepped in to help. I remember his mother once asking him, 'What's the point of working like this if you don't even have time to eat your meals properly?' He was struggling to balance his roles as an employee, husband, father, brother and son.

Anand was slowly growing unhappy with his work, even though his job title, salary and bonuses were improving. He couldn't reconcile the company's practice of maximising profits by underpaying small-scale industries for their goods and services, as it went against his core values. Additionally, he felt disheartened that he was unable to pursue his passion.

It had been more than six years since they had relocated. Their daughter was now in 9th grade, and their son in 6th.

Though Anand grew increasingly frustrated with work, he continued as other organisations more aligned with his passion offering relatively lower pay and were not well-known names in the industry. After much contemplation, he finally decided to return to his previous company—the one he believed truly reflected his dream job, and values.

As Anand began persuading Preethi to leave her job and relocate to their former town, Preethi proposed a different approach. She suggested that Anand go ahead on his own at first, as she might not be able to find a job in their old town immediately. Additionally, she expressed concerns about disrupting their children's education by switching schools at that point. Acknowledging the limited availability of interior design agencies in the old town, Anand encouraged Preethi to consider starting her own agency, assuring her of his full support in establishing the business.

However, Preethi countered by suggesting that Anand could consider taking a lower-paid job available locally. This way, both of them could continue to work and earn, with minimal disruption to their family life. Anand felt unsupported and even insulted by her suggestions, while Preethi had also begun to grow stubborn and was unwilling to explore other possibilities.

Discussions slowly escalated into arguments, and minor disagreements turned into serious fights. Anand continued to struggle with finding a well-paid job that matched his interests, while Preethi remained preoccupied with managing their home, teenage children, and her work commitments. Their communication broke down, leading to growing bitterness and resentment.

Eventually, Preethi and Anand took the painful decision to end their marriage.

This turn of events came as a shock to their parents, friends, and extended family, who had always been proud and happy for them. They tried their best to help improve the situation, but could ultimately do nothing but witness everything in helplessness and pain.

Now, Anand continues to work at the same company, though he has lost his wit and charm. Preethi has moved to a small rented house with their daughter, but she struggles with depression and is currently on medication. Their son lives with Anand and spends weekends with his mother and sister.

Both children are grappling with health issues, having withdrawn from all extracurricular activities. Their studies have also begun to suffer. What a tragedy.

My eyes are filled with tears as I write this account of Anand, Preethi and their children. Anand and Preethi are not alone here. There are many people around us experiencing similar shades of pain and agony.

The Most Important Job

What was the turning point?

What caused the shift from good to bad so suddenly?

Despite having other opportunities in the same town that more closely matched his interests, Anand chose not to pursue them. Was it the brand he worked for, the salary, or the status that outweighed his real aspirations? Or was it just fear of the unknown that held him back? And what was most important to Preethi—her job, financial stability, the children, or something else entirely? Could this have been a typical midlife crisis?

It appears they couldn't recognise, internalise and prioritise what truly mattered to them: the choices for success and happiness.

Had Anand and Preethi stepped back to consider the following perspectives, the outcome could have been different.

- What truly matters to me at this moment? Is it a job that aligns with my interests, a respected title, a better salary, my family, or recognition in society?

- If other priorities outweigh the desire for a role aligned with my passion, should I consider postponing a change until I'm better prepared? Where do I stand at present in terms of skills and readiness?

- Why do I expect someone else to sacrifice something important for the sake of my dream? Am I willing to do the same for them?

- My financial stability, living conditions, family, and social life have turned out to be far better than I had once imagined, which were once my top priorities. Is it worth putting all of that at risk for the one thing I now hold most dear?

- Even if we aren't making progress towards our original goals, why not continue striving to be an inspiring father, mother, son, daughter, brother, sister, uncle, or aunt? And perhaps, with some time and effort, even rediscover love as partners?

As humans, we have the potential to achieve remarkable feats or make terrible mistakes. It depends entirely on the choices we make, not the situations in which we find ourselves. If you don't understand yourself, failure will be hard to overcome, and success will be even harder for both you and those around you.

You can't do any good if you don't feel good. You must first find success and happiness—only then can you extend it to your family, work, and the world around you. Not the other way round.

Growing up in your parents' home until your teenage years can be fun, as you typically receive everything for free there. School and college life revolve largely around study, with considerable support and guidance. But succeeding at work demands a wide range of skills, and you're largely on your own to build them.

The dating phase may be exciting and carefree, whereas marriage and parenting require considerable commitment and effort. Life in later years is an entirely different experience. You need to continuously learn, unlearn, and adapt to navigate and thrive in ever-evolving circumstances.

If you believe you're always right, you'll miss valuable opportunities to learn and grow. Each stage of life demands a different version of you, and it is essential to consciously grow into that role to be successful, happy, and joyful.

It could be vastly different from your former self, and you may be unable to anticipate or prepare for it. Such is life's nature. No one else can do it for you. Even if someone is willing to make a sacrifice on your behalf, it will still fall short of meeting your requirements. The change must come from within, not from outside.

No school will teach you how to master this. Conventional self-help books, motivational workshops, and personal development courses, management or leadership training, or spiritual talks may offer little help in this context. This isn't about quick solutions, personality shortcuts, networking tactics, stakeholder engagement techniques, or people-management strategies.

Many organisations and individuals invest significant time, effort, and money in such training programs. However, these often lead to only minor, superficial changes. In fact, research indicates they may occasionally have a modest negative impact on personal performance and productivity.

They will not be effective long-term unless they align with your authentic self and future aspirations. They may provide a brief surge of motivation, but the effect typically fades within days, leaving you exactly where you began.

To truly transform, you must undergo fundamental shifts in your thoughts, beliefs, and values, which shape how you view the world and interact with everything around you, both living and non-living. Often, you may need to unlearn more than you learn. Sometimes, what you're desperately clinging to may be exactly what you need to let go of.

It's not an easy task, but it's entirely achievable. A few months of focused effort, discipline, and consistency can lead to remarkable changes within you.

Each of us, consciously or unconsciously, guards our own gate of change, which can only be opened from within—by you alone. Others may only influence you to open it through knowledge and encouragement, not through force or persuasion.

As an author, that is my sole motivation for you through this book!

Step 1

Discover Yourself

Love what you do, or don't do it at all. The only way to reach that point is by discovering who you truly are and gaining clarity about what genuinely matters to you.

Let's take the first step towards building your best life!

To succeed in life, you are often advised to discover yourself, prioritise what truly matters, love what you do, and pursue your dreams. But if you do not know how to go about it, it can feel disheartening.

As with any endeavour, it's essential to internalise clear goals and essential elements for success before taking action. This not only improves the likelihood of success but also makes the journey easier, more efficient, and enjoyable.

In this case, it's about understanding human nature and its makeup, to define success, to internalise what brings true happiness, and to learn how to sustain it for a joyful life.

Boiled vegetables!

They are so easy to make and so nutritious! With a couple of slices of bread, they make a complete meal. I love having them for breakfast.

I often enjoy it at breakfast buffets while travelling, although I rarely see it on typical hotel menus. I have tried making it at home, but I have never quite managed to get the same taste. I've experimented with broccoli, cauliflower, beans, carrots, cucumber, button mushrooms, green chillies and red chillies—by adjusting the quantities and combinations, and even trying different cooking oils. Yet despite its simplicity, I've never quite managed to get it right.

Every time I had it at hotels, I meticulously analysed the proportions of the different vegetables, how well they were cooked, and any additional ingredients, but nothing seemed to warrant a second look or adjustment. Unfortunately, I couldn't uncover the secret from cookbooks or online sources either.

It was during a work trip to Mumbai in India that I had a breakthrough. After a long morning run, I rushed to the restaurant for breakfast.

You know what I was thinking? Would there be boiled vegetables in the breakfast buffet?

And there it was, it was one of the best portions of boiled vegetables I'd ever tasted. As usual, I examined it thoroughly but couldn't spot anything different from what I make at home.

I called the waiter over and asked, 'May I speak to the chef who prepared this, please?'

'Is there a problem, sir?' the waiter asked, a hint of panic in his voice.

'It's brilliant. I just can't seem to make it like this at home. I would really appreciate the chance to speak to your chef,' I explained.

'Let me check, sir,' the waiter replied, visibly relieved.

He went straight into the kitchen and returned shortly, saying, 'Sorry, sir. He's very busy until breakfast service is over.'

I asked him to inform the chef that I was happy to wait until he was free.

I sat at the table for over an hour after finishing my breakfast, reading the newspaper and checking my e-mails.

Around 10 o'clock, the person I'd been eagerly waiting for arrived. When the student is ready, the teacher appears.

'Yes, sir. How can I help you?' he asked in a soft voice.

I stood up, bowed to him and said, 'Sorry to trouble you. The boiled vegetables were exceptional today. I often make it at home, but never quite achieve this taste. What's your secret?'

He blushed with pride and replied, 'Nothing special, sir. Would you mind sharing how you prepare them at home?'

I knew I was speaking to an expert, but I explained everything in detail: the types of vegetables I use, the size at which I cut them, how I cook them separately, the various oils I've tried for seasoning, and so on. He listened patiently to the entire explanation and then remarked,

'You're doing everything I do, sir, but with just a few minor changes.'

'Use butter, not any other oils, for the seasoning. Secondly, don't use chillies, but freshly ground pepper. One more thing, sir, add the pepper only after turning off the heat,' he advised.

I felt relieved and happy, but was still doubtful until I tried it. I bought all the required vegetables on my way home and cooked them the same day.

It was incredible! It worked. What a taste!

The two ingredients, along with a minor change in the process, made all the difference. It seemed so simple once the solution was found. Of course, it required acknowledging the problem, focused attention, persistent effort, and seeking help to fix it—like everything else in life.

Human life has the highest potential and possibility compared to any other life on the planet. It is nature's greatest triumph, the result of its valiant evolutionary journey. Animals are happy and content if they eat, mate, and sleep. That is the definition of success for a mouse, monkey, elephant, or even the lion—the king of the jungle. But human success goes beyond these primal instincts.

The key differences between humans and animals lie in self-awareness and in the ability to think, imagine, and transform—not just once but repeatedly—demonstrating boundless potential for growth and change. This drives individuals to pursue their unique aspirations and objectives.

Unique aspirations?

Yes—the very pursuit of success, happiness, and meaning in life.

Whenever you said or meant, 'I'm not like that,' 'It's not important to me,' or 'Let me chase my dream,' you were also, in some way, contemplating:

Who am I?

What makes me?

And why am I here—right?

You are made up of just three ingredients: your body, your mind, and YOU. Nothing more.

Your Body

The physical structure you possess serves as a tool for all actions in the real world. All animals, from mice to monkeys, including you, have similar organs that essentially perform the same functions.

It is akin to a computer's hardware, housing numerous interconnected components for sensing, processing, and storage. Since you cannot alter its fundamental composition, it is rightly called hardware.

We will explore this in detail and learn how to care for it and make the best use of it—in Step 3.

Your Mind

The sum of all your life experiences to date—your beliefs, likes, dislikes, and indifference towards everything around you.

It's akin to computer software, consisting of written and stored instructions necessary for operation. Unlike hardware, these instructions can be modified by the user—hence the term 'software'.

We will explore this in detail and learn how to master your mind and get the most out of it—in Step 2.

YOU

The part of your preferences that forms the foundation and expression of your life. It is as unique to you as your DNA or fingerprint. From this point forward, let's refer to it as 'YOU' to distinguish it from the composite 'you' that comprises the three components. This helps avoid using other terminologies.

It's akin to a computer's firmware, outlining the fundamental characteristics of the machine. Installed permanently during manufacture in a specific memory location, it is rarely altered thereafter, earning it the name 'firmware'.

Success in life does not require understanding how the entire world operates, but rather knowing what works best for you. It is all about you—understanding the three elements that make up your being and making the best of them.

Everything you need is already within you, but the right guidance can make the journey easier.

I am here to help you master the craft.

Let's dive deep into who you are, what truly matters to you, and why you're here, and begin your journey of self-discovery!

Your Birth and You

Let's start at the very beginning, when your life journey begins. It all started when a sperm, a male cell, embarked on its journey and merged with the ovum, a mature female cell, giving rise to an embryo. This embryo began to grow, eventually forming your body.

Within six to seven weeks, a neural network and memory begin to form in the foetus, signifying the beginning of life, and they stabilise by around three months.

And there you were—born into the world!

Of course, you had to wait a few more months within your mother's womb before you were ready to enter and thrive in the outside world.

Your body and neural network continue to develop based on various factors, including the food your mother consumes, her physical and mental health, the influences of her environment, and her thoughts and emotions. If you're considering having children, internalise it as a significant responsibility because the well-being and potential of a new life depend greatly on how you conduct your own life.

Epigenetics studies shows that your consistent actions can influence how your genes are expressed—though they don't alter your DNA sequence. It affects your physical health and mental conditioning—and these changes can be passed on to future generations through gene expression.

Every life on this planet often exceeds our imagination and tests the limits of our intelligence. Beyond the miraculous functioning of your body and mind, consider the magical role of your DNA. It not only preserves your unique traits but also carries the legacy of generations before you. And the fact that you can be distinguished from millions of people by the unique codes on your fingertips is truly remarkable.

There is no one like you, and there will never be anyone like you again. A truly original creation!

Consider the incredible journey of life that begins within a seed, patiently awaiting its moment to transform into a plant. As the seed comes into contact with soil and water, it begins to sprout, with delicate green leaves emerging from the hard ground. If the seed lacks life, it simply decomposes and becomes part of the soil.

Whether it's a groundnut seed becoming a groundnut plant or a pumpkin seed growing into a pumpkin creeper, all the instructions for their growth are encoded within the seed itself. No confusion, no errors.

With the help of Mother Nature, sunlight, and water, the plant or creeper continues to grow. Flowers bloom, fruits form, and they carry the seeds of the next generation. Eventually, the plant or creeper reaches the end of its life cycle. Soil and water that supported its growth decompose it, returning its nutrients to the earth. The new seeds await their chance to sprout and begin the cycle anew.

The intricate and magical functioning of life always astounds us with its complexity and beauty. What we know is very little.

According to the laws of physics, energy cannot be created or destroyed; it simply changes from one form to another. Consider the water we drink—it's as old as the Earth itself. The water we consume today contains molecules that have been recycled by nature for billions of years.

Not just water, but everything around us. The air we breathe, the fruit we eat, and every atom in our bodies are as old as, if not older than, planet Earth.

There has never been a time in the past when you, others, and everything around you did not exist. Similarly, there will never be a time in the future when you and they won't exist. Nature continuously recycles, repackages, and repurposes everything. Forms, names, and illusions only get destroyed. Nothing else changes.

Over the past century, modern science has made significant strides in understanding life through research and reverse engineering. This knowledge has immense value for humanity, especially in terms of survival and combating illness.

On the other hand, spiritual gurus, particularly those from countries like India, have developed a profound understanding of life through centuries of observation and perception. Their insights, rooted in ancient wisdom, remain invaluable even today as they offer a holistic approach to life.

They utilise their bodies as sensors and their perception to decode life, recognising that nature has encoded everything within each of us. From this understanding originated the Karma philosophy. If they were hallucinating, those experiences would not have been perceived as real even by a second person.

However, their value and acceptance persist today due to their consistent experiences over thousands of years by a wider group of people. Scientific evidence also relies on consistent results over multiple observations involving a broader set of individuals, correct?

Let's explore both perspectives. Feel free to choose whichever resonates with you, as our goal is not to favour one over the other but to gain a deeper understanding of how life operates and manifests.

Often, we encounter two groups of people: those who blindly believe in something and those who question every aspect of it. Both approaches can prevent anyone from getting the best out of them. The best course of action is to understand them, derive insights, and build upon them for the benefit of ourselves and the world around us.

Let's begin by examining the scientific view first.

The Scientific View

You had a body when you began your life as a foetus in your mother's womb. Within six to seven weeks, a neural network and memory begin to form in the foetus.

The majority of your memory initially consists of genetic memory. By three months, your body, neural network, and memory typically reach a stable state. If they don't, a miscarriage may occur, resulting in the loss of the embryo. This is why most miscarriages during this period are attributed to genetic issues.

Yes, you have successfully navigated through that critical phase in your life, and here you are!

Your physical well-being after birth is influenced by the foods you consume and the exercise you engage in. At the same time, your neural network and memory shape the characteristics of your mind.

The billions of neurons that form trillions of connections with each other, along with your memory, make you uniquely who you are. Everything you've ever seen, heard, touched, tasted, smelled, been told, or learnt contributes to shaping your mind.

Your reactions and responses to everything are determined solely by your mind. Whether it's interactions with people, animals, plants, objects, or concepts like religion, politics, wealth, power, or fame, everything manifests within you uniquely based on your mindset.

Certainly, your mind will continue to evolve throughout your life, shaped by your experiences, forming new neural pathways and dissolving some existing ones, until your last breath. Some aspects of your mind will remain relatively unchanged, holding significant importance to you, much like your unique fingerprint or DNA.

In essence, it is distinctly YOU!

Karma Philosophy

'Karma' is a word from the Sanskrit language that has been widely referenced across the globe for centuries and continues to be widely used even today. Sanskrit is also one of the oldest languages in the world, used for writing many Indian spiritual scriptures.

According to the Karma philosophy, life is perceived as a succession of cycles that continue until all of one's desires are fulfilled. The sum of an individual's actions in both their current and previous lives is referred to as their Karma.

Let's revisit the beginning. Within six to seven weeks after conception, a neural network and memory begin to form in the foetus. Initially, this memory is predominantly karmic memory.

What is karmic memory?

Karmic memory comprises everything from one's current life and past lives, existing in the form of conscious, subconscious, and unconscious tendencies.

According to the Karma philosophy, your current life is seen as an extension of your previous life. In your previous life, you experienced death when your body could no longer sustain its vital processes due to factors such as old age, illness, or other circumstances.

It's possible that you did not fulfill all your desires, and some may not have even been addressed. Your karmic memory, the essence of who you are, or the YOU, encompasses this unfulfilled residual set of significant matters for you.

You are given a new opportunity to fulfil your desires in this situation. You understand that without a physical body and a rational mind, you cannot function in the real world. Therefore, to start a new life and pursue your unfulfilled desires, you will manifest as a foetus in a woman's womb, equipped with a neural network and your karmic memory.

This process is akin to installing firmware, which is rarely altered, onto the raw hardware of a computer during its manufacturing process. Of course, the self-learning software necessary for your operation will be set up and updated later.

In this process, the man and the woman who created the body for YOU become incredibly important figures in your life—your father and your mother. They are expected to support your desires for as long as you need them. This is why YOU chose to associate with them or were placed in the most suitable environment to begin your new life.

However, it's important not to expect perfect solutions from them because they, too are navigating life's challenges while assisting you in moving forward. Moreover, they are yesterday's people striving to prepare today's generation for tomorrow.

Accept whatever support you receive from them with utmost respect and gratitude, as they often set aside their own needs and desires to fulfil yours.

If you're a parent, it's crucial to ensure that your children receive the same treatment. This is your primary responsibility and duty to them. Remember, your children are not meant for your enjoyment, pride, or to fulfil your requirements, but rather to pursue their desires with your support.

This will demand a significant portion of your time, effort, and finances, and you may not receive anything in return. They may not even visit you as they grow up and get busy with their own lives. This is the law of nature and applies to all life on the planet. If you cannot accept this reality and responsibility, it's best to avoid having children, as it can make life challenging for both you and your children.

It doesn't mean you should give them everything they ask for. Naturally, you need to hold their hands when they're young, so they don't get lost in the crowd. As they grow older, you must gradually let go and allow them to embrace and experience the world around them. However, you can't control the outcomes because you can't control the world or how your child interacts with it. Everyone has their own unique experience with how the world works.

A mother and her daughter were travelling in an air-conditioned compartment of a long-distance train. The girl appeared to be around eight years old and was seated in the middle seat of a three-seat row, with the mother in the aisle seat.

A middle-aged man sat in the window seat, engrossed in reading a book. When I boarded the train and took the seat opposite him, he greeted me with a smile and said hello.

The girl was often seen eating while engrossed in playing video games on her tablet, while the mother was mostly occupied with her phone. The girl appeared to be visibly overweight and lethargic.

Whenever the train catering staff passed by, she would ask her mother to buy something, and the mother would oblige. However, when the mother refused her request for bright red sugar candy, the girl persisted in asking for it and eventually began crying loudly. It was disturbing for all the nearby passengers.

'Excuse me, would it be possible for my daughter to sit there? It might help calm her down,' the mother requested of the man at the window seat.

He paused his reading, eyebrows raised, glanced at the mother and the crying daughter. With a gentle smile, he responded.

'I don't mind, but perhaps not at the moment. It's important for your daughter to understand that she can't always get everything she wants, and that the world doesn't always go as she wishes.'

I'm not sure if the girl grasped the sentiment, but her mother seemed to. It lingered in my thoughts for a while, until I found myself once again captivated by the swiftly passing scenes outside, gazing through the window.

You may be contemplating how a foetus in a woman's womb receives YOU as life energy.

According to quantum physics, everything in existence consists of 99.999 percent energy and only 0.001 percent matter. This means that every atom in your body, as well as in the vast universe, is primarily energy and interconnected.

There are numerous types of energy on the planet that many of us may not be able to perceive, quantify, or fully comprehend. Indian 'Pranic' healing harnesses a person's life energy to heal someone else without physical contact.

A similar concept is employed in the Japanese healing practice of 'Reiki.' Practitioners are able to work both in close proximity and across distances, much like speaking on the phone with someone located elsewhere in the world. Even though they are far away from you, you can still make them happy, sad, angry, or depressed by talking to them over the phone, right?

It is possible because electromagnetic energy carrying your words travels across vast distances through the air from your phone to the other person. Moreover, this energy is selectively directed only to the person of your choice among millions of people.

Isn't it possible for any other type of energy also to work in similar ways?

The crow holds significant importance in Karma philosophy. It appears that crows can detect various energy forms in their environment. For example, they often make a lot of noise hours before an earthquake.

Additionally, there's a belief that when a crow sings a particular tune around your home, it signifies that you will have a visitor. According to this belief, the crow sings in a different key when it senses the energies of the visitor as they prepare to visit you.

Let's consider these as possibilities, because believing that what we don't know or can't know doesn't exist can be a significant limitation.

The life you're living now started with a new body capable of fulfilling your desires. But what if you die without achieving them in this life? Another chance will come to YOU. This cycle repeats until YOU fulfil all your desires, depleting all your Karma. This progression unfolds through various cycles of life and death.

You might not need another life if you fulfil all your desires in this one, because in doing so, YOU cease to exist, which means you achieve *Moksha*—Sanskrit for liberation from the cycle of birth and death. *Moksha* is considered the ultimate goal of human life according to Karma philosophy.

Purushartha in Sanskrit, which means the objective of human life, articulates this progression as *Dharma, Artha, Kama,* and *Moksha*. *Dharma*, or righteousness, signifies your responsibilities toward yourself, your family, and society. To fulfil these responsibilities, you need to earn *Artha*, or wealth. With wealth, you can fulfil your *Kama*, or desires. As your desires are satisfied, you achieve *Moksha*, or liberation.

What will occur if you fulfil all your desires in your current life well in advance?

Even though you may feel like leaving your body at any time, you know that you won't die until your body wears out and can no longer perform necessary life functions.

What will you do till you die since all your desires are already fulfilled?

That will be the best thing that can happen to you. You'll be content, fearless, and open to anything, enjoying true liberation and ultimate freedom. You will broaden your horizons, accept everything, and dedicate yourself to greater missions of selfless service.

That is what *Sannyasa* in Sanskrit means. It's not an act or specific attire, but a state where you have only your body and mind, and you work for the benefit of society at large because YOU or your desires have ceased to exist.

There would be more love, compassion, creativity, and productivity and a lot less sadness, rudeness, mediocrity, jealousy, and hatred in the world if there were more people who behaved in that way. The world as a single family or *Vasudhaiva Kutumbakam* in Sanskrit.

To help you fulfil some of your desires more quickly than others in this lifetime, your desires are further divided into immediate and later according to the Karma philosophy. If you're not adding any new ones as you go about your life, you can work on the second priority list if they're still important, once you've finished the first one.

The entirety of your unfinished Karma is known as Sanchita Karma, the portion with the highest priority is known as Prarabdha Karma, and any additional Karma you may add is known as Agami Karma.

Prarabdha Karma shapes the direction of your life, while Sanchita Karma remains dormant as unconscious tendencies towards various things. This differs from person to person, depending on what matters most to them. As a result, even identical twins exhibit different desires, preferences, and behaviours not to mention other children of the same parents.

Remember that you were created for a purpose: to fulfil your desires, which are unique and important to you, regardless of what the world may suggest otherwise.

Self-awareness or conscious living involves delving deeply into your Karma and actively working to resolve it sooner rather than waiting for it to unfold gradually across multiple lifetimes. It means prioritising and addressing everything significant to you at the earliest opportunity. By doing so, you can potentially liberate yourself from your Karma in fewer lifetimes, perhaps even in this one. May this be the reality for you and for every other person on earth.

Your actions—whether taken, avoided, or planned—and their consequences, whether good or bad, are entirely your responsibility. That is the essence and significance of Karma philosophy. It's up to you to determine your own destiny, fate is when you fail to create your destiny.

The Real You

I'm not sure if the Karma philosophy or the scientific viewpoint resonated with you. But it doesn't really matter. Both offer insights into life's mysteries and valuable perspectives on what matters most to you personally, and ultimately, your life is about striving to realise those things.

Does it matter whether you are a male or female in this context?

Do desires have a gender? It sounds funny, doesn't it?

If you're considering the biological differences between male and female bodies, they exist solely for reproductive purposes.

For similar reasons, women often excel in organising and maintaining order and are more attuned to sensing and responding to threats, driven by a strong sense of responsibility that stems from their nurturing traits, more so than men at the psychological level.

In the last massive tsunami that struck the southeastern coastal areas of India, claiming thousands of lives in just twenty minutes, women and children comprised the majority of the victims. Women were swept into the sea because, unlike men, they were unwilling to flee from the gigantic, roaring waves without their children. It was heartbreaking to witness many of them perish while holding their children tightly.

The fact that you are a man or a woman does not matter—but your masculine and feminine qualities do.

Masculine traits such as being analytical, logical, decisive, assertive, independent, individualistic, and self-assured are often associated with men.

Conversely, feminine qualities like intuition, creativity, receptiveness, nurturing, grace, sensitivity, and compassion are often attributed to women.

Nothing about these traits should make anyone feel superior or inferior, happy, or sad. That's the rule of nature, which applies to all living things on the planet, not just humans.

According to the Karma philosophy, one may go through multiple male and female lives to fulfil all their desires.

Do you want to know about your past lives if you believe in the Karma philosophy? Does that information matter to you or provide any help?

You might already be struggling with the memories from your current life if you're still unable to let go of something that happened years ago and continue to feel sad, angry, or agitated about it. Even if the other person(s) involved have moved on and forgotten about it, you might even be harboring thoughts of revenge.

Now, imagine carrying memories from a past life. Do you think you could handle that too? Or would it only make things worse?

Imagine that you had children in your previous life and you recognise them in your current life. You might see them enjoying the wealth you left behind, perhaps even living in your old bungalow in a prime locality. How would you feel if you're currently struggling to meet your basic needs? Would you feel comfortable asking them for help? And do you think they would help you if you asked?

Living in the past consumes a lot of your energy, leaving you worn out and less productive. Remember, the life ahead of you is far more important than the one behind you. Move on.

Ramayana and Mahabharata are two of the most significant ancient Indian epics. The Bhagavad Gita, a revered text, is a part of the Mahabharata.

While the Ramayana emphasises the obligations and duties of individuals, the Mahabharata focuses on the righteous performance of those duties. These epics cover a wide range of topics and provide timeless role models for everyone to contemplate and emulate.

Karna, a celebrated warrior in the Mahabharata, faced challenging circumstances from birth. Despite being born into a royal family, his mother left him due to external pressures, and he was raised by charioteers. However, Karna excelled in archery and emerged as a formidable warrior.

Recognising his prowess, King Duryodhana appointed Karna as the battlefield commander and assigned Salya, a capable King, as his charioteer. Duryodhana's decision aimed to honour Karna's abilities and uplift his morale, despite his humble background.

Salya wasn't very happy about serving as the charioteer to Karna, given Karna's humble origins, despite his exceptional skills as a warrior and his critical role in the ongoing war.

During the intense battle, when Karna's chariot wheel became stuck in the ground, Salya neglected his duty to assist, leaving Karna to dismount and resolve the issue alone, despite his primary role as a warrior in combat.

Arjuna, Karna's opponent, had the opportunity to kill Karna at that point, with Krishna serving as his charioteer and moral compass.

Despite being born into a royal family and possessing far greater capabilities than Arjuna, Krishna was comfortable serving as his charioteer, standing by him in his time of need and at a critical juncture in the war.

What matters is who you are today, not who you were.

Demystifying Success

Success, in its essence, is straightforward and simple. It is about being happy and joyful, not just for yourself—but for all life on the planet.

Happiness and joy—are they the same?

Not exactly.

Happiness often arises in response to external factors such as people, places, things, conditions, and circumstances. It is transient and usually tied to specific reasons.

Joy, on the other hand, comes from self-realisation, a sense of purpose, inner peace, and fulfilment. Unlike happiness, joy is enduring and can exist regardless of external circumstances.

For many, success is equated with attaining high status, building a strong reputation, accumulating wealth, finding the right partner, and raising their children to be successful. Ironically, these achievements often fail to sustain lasting happiness in people's lives.

In recent decades, there has been a proliferation of choices in various aspects of life, including food, relationships, careers, comfort, and convenience. However, despite these expanded choices, indicators such as health, divorce rates, wealth, and overall happiness have not improved; in fact, they have worsened.

Interestingly, even with greater freedom and power, men are not necessarily happier than women. Similarly, while younger individuals may enjoy more opportunities and better physical health, older people often report higher levels of happiness—even in the face of health challenges.

People living in colder climates often believe that those in warmer regions are luckier and happier. People in developing countries often view those in developed nations as more fortunate or happier. People who consider themselves less attractive may think the attractive ones are happier. Unmarried people often believe married life brings more happiness, and poor people often assume wealthy people are happier—all of which are far from the truth.

The truth is humans are born happy and possess an innate desire to remain that way throughout life.

A four-year-old laughs hundreds of times a day on average. As we grow older, we gradually learn to be unhappy. Our education, work, relationships, and life experiences often dull that natural joy. I hope you still manage a few good laughs each day—if not hundreds!

Ancient wisdom and modern research have converged on a similar formula for what shapes human happiness.

Roughly 50 percent comes from mental conditioning—your baseline level of happiness. About 20 percent is influenced by material comforts, and the remaining 30 percent depends on personal choices. Think of these as relative contributors rather than fixed percentages.

Let us delve into each aspect in detail.

You know the happiness that comes from achieving something—but how long does it last? Often you adapt to the new situation and quickly return to your usual baseline level of happiness, right?

Consider the top five things that you believe would bring you lasting happiness if achieved. Now think back—chances are, you've already accomplished more than five from a similar list in the past. Yet, you may not feel significantly happier than you did back then.

Whether it was graduating from school, landing a job, getting promoted, buying a car, moving into a new home, getting married to someone attractive, having children, or hitting other milestones. About 50 percent of your happiness stays relatively constant regardless of the ups and downs of life. That's your mental conditioning.

Only 20 percent of your happiness comes from material comforts—things like your home, car, job, money, jewelry, clothes, gadgets, power, beauty, and fame. Ironically, although this holds the least weight in the happiness equation, it often gets the most of your time and attention. Isn't that true?

The quality of your life isn't determined by the size of your home, but by how you live in it. Similarly, a fancy office will not drive your success, but the work you do there. A sophisticated phone won't foster meaningful relationships, but the quality of your conversations. Likewise, a pricey car or first-class ticket will not significantly enhance your journey as much as where you're going, with whom, and for what purpose.

The rest lies entirely in your mind. Only in your mind!

I'm not suggesting you ignore these needs altogether, but do not let them define your worth as an individual. Research consistently shows that those who prioritise materialistic goals tend to be less happy, and even less healthy than those who focus on less materialistic pursuits.

Wealth is like salt water; the more you drink, the thirstier you become. The same goes for fame and power. They are like any other addiction, often more damaging than smoking or alcohol.

I'm not saying you can't buy happiness with money, but it depends on what you choose to buy.

Instead of spending on a fancy villa, high-end car, or advanced gadget—especially when many of their features go unused—you might consider spending your money on family vacations, gatherings with friends, a fitness regimen for yourself, an appliance or tool that makes your life easier, or making charitable contributions. These are less affected by the adaptation principle and can bring you happiness that lasts longer.

In addition to the effects of adaptation, the declining value of expensive possessions—along with the effort and cost required to maintain and update them—can further diminish your happiness.

Money can help you meet your needs and take away one of your worries about not having money. Just one of your concerns. Of course, without money, you wouldn't have many of the things you enjoy today, including the place you live, the clothes you wear, and the food you eat.

Money itself is neither inherently good nor bad; it simply amplifies your existing qualities. If you're a good person, you'll likely use money wisely, leading to positive outcomes. Conversely, if you're inclined toward negative behaviour, you may misuse money, inviting negative consequences.

The same applies to fame or power. Each of these offers opportunities to help, employ, influence, and positively impact the lives of others. Use them to make a meaningful difference in your own life and in the world around you.

The remaining 30 percent of happiness comes from your choices—activities you engage in willingly. Whether it's your hobbies, nurturing good relationships, contributing to a cause, or doing work you truly enjoy, these endeavours encourage deep engagement, fostering happiness.

The happiest individuals aren't necessarily those who have everything, but those who are deeply engaged in meaningful pursuits and love what they do.

Love What You Do

You often become unhappy when you are not able to do something important to you, right?

Doing what you love will make you happy and joyful, but no one's life will always be that way, anywhere on the planet. Life is unpredictable and will throw numerous challenges at you. They may excite you, challenge you, overwhelm you, or even break you—this applies to everyone—whether rich, poor, or even a king or a queen.

You might have a strong passion for serving as a soldier, defending your country, your family, and others, but you can't choose the war. You might not always be able to do what you love, but what matters most in your life at that moment.

Will you give it top priority and your best effort if it's important to you? Yes—correct?

For example, even if you love photography, you might work at a shopping mall to support yourself because, at that point in your life, that's what matters most. In that case, can you dislike what you're doing or not 'love what you do?'

Though the end result is the same, I hope you understand the subtle distinction between 'doing what you love' and 'loving what you do.'

'Doing what you love' refers to pursuing activities aligned with your passions and interests, while 'loving what you do' involves finding value and fulfillment in the tasks at hand, even if they were not your initial preference.

A disciple once struggled to finish his modest snack before praying and asked the master if he could eat it while praying.

'Do nothing else while praying,' the master replied. The disciple bowed and entered the prayer room.

On another occasion, the master noticed the disciples chatting while snacking before prayer. 'You should be present with yourself while eating,' he advised.

Intrigued, a disciple asked, 'Master, can we pray while eating?'

'Of course—you can pray anytime,' the master affirmed.

As illustrated in both scenarios, eating and praying are performed simultaneously, but it is the internalisation of these actions that makes the true difference.

Painting a canvas and painting a wall can be equally creative, enjoyable, or boring. You will experience stress if what is important to you feels distant from what you're doing. Your motivation and commitment then require constant effort, which isn't sustainable.

However, if what you're doing is perceived as closely aligned with what's important to you, it becomes immersive and energising. You will love what you do, give it your all, bring out the best in yourself, and experience happiness and joy.

Love what you do—or don't do it at all. I call it 'LoWyD' for short.

The only way to get there is by gaining clarity about yourself.

Discover yourself!

Needs and Desires

Do you always feel unhappy when you can't do something?

Not necessarily—it depends on how important it is to you, correct?

Let's categorise them as your needs and desires. Yes, we'll stick with these terms consistently throughout the book.

Your needs will mostly revolve around yourself, your immediate family, or close friends—like securing a good education for yourself or a loved one, buying a car or house, repaying loans, or even providing necessities like food and clothing for your family.

These needs are fundamentally tied to your survival and well-being. Even though many of them are done for someone else, they ultimately contribute to your own happiness—otherwise, you're unlikely to pursue them.

Many years ago, my daughter and I went together to a bicycle shop to buy a new bicycle she had been asking for. To my surprise, it turned out to be much pricier than I had expected. While exploring cheaper options with the shopkeeper, I casually mentioned that the same amount could buy me a better mobile phone—something I had been postponing for a while.

The shopkeeper replied, 'Certainly, Sir, but your daughter can't sit on the phone and ride it.'

It made me pause and think—what is it that I would truly love to do now? And she rode her new bicycle home.

Your desires, unlike your needs, extend beyond yourself and basic survival—like helping others access basic education, ensuring no one around you goes hungry, protecting the environment, creating jobs, developing products or services that make life easier and happier for others, or enabling faster, safer, and more convenient travel.

The product or service you choose to deliver is often just a means to fulfil your desires. For example, a coffee shop or mobile app may be your way to create a space for people to connect. Books, theatre, or training programs could be how you share knowledge. Organic farms, diet plans, or fitness gear all promote healthier living. Affordable housing, microloans, or low-cost food to help meet basic needs. Medical devices, doctors, nurses, pharmaceuticals—all save lives.

The key is to choose your path based on your strengths—skills you already have or are ready to develop—not just what's trendy or popular. After all, every meaningful pursuit aims to serve others' needs while helping you fulfill your own desires.

As you know, Anand aspired to become a doctor. His dream was to offer essential medical care, especially in remote villages. He wanted to make a real difference in the lives of people who often had to spend a lot of time, effort, and money travelling to cities for life-saving treatment—disrupting many areas of their lives in the process.

Eventually, he chose to pursue biomedical engineering, specialising in medical device development, to fulfil that dream. Sure, his job title would be 'Engineer,' not 'Doctor,' but that was unrelated to his desire.

Your desires will be your orientation and purpose in life. A life's purpose isn't something you invent—it's something you discover. If you don't, you can become distracted, lethargic, and seek constant stimulation—an endlessly restless thrill-seeker.

Even if it's the most delicious food, how much can you really eat? Even if the music is truly melodious, how long can you listen for? Even if you're gazing at the most beautiful scene, how long can you keep watching? Even if you're with the most beautiful woman or the most handsome man, you'll eventually feel exhausted after a while, right?

If you focus only on your needs, your desires may be sidelined, leaving you with a sense of sacrificing what truly matters for what's merely essential—often leading to dissatisfaction. On the other hand, if you give all your attention to your desires, your basic needs might get neglected, upsetting your family or friends who rely on you to meet those needs—again, leading to unhappiness.

To resolve this dilemma, a practical approach is to prioritise your needs first. Once your basic needs are taken care of, you'll naturally begin to focus on your desires and work toward them.

However, if for any reason you're unable to pursue your desires even after meeting your needs, it can become frustrating and diminish your happiness—as we saw in Anand's case. That's because we're wired to feel most fulfilled when we contribute to something beyond ourselves. It's natural—acting otherwise is difficult.

As flight safety instructions remind us, 'In case of cabin decompression, oxygen masks will drop automatically. Pull the mask towards you, secure it over your nose, and breathe normally. If you are travelling with an infant or someone needing assistance, secure your mask first before helping others.' This instruction emphasises the importance of taking care of yourself first because if you don't, you may be unable to help yourself or others.

Spending less than you earn, avoiding consumer debt, saving money, and investing wisely can all accelerate your journey towards financial independence. Remember, true wealth lies not just in what you earn, but in what you don't spend. It provides you with options, flexibility, and financial growth. However, it's equally important to invest in yourself—to build your skills and strengthen your abilities to excel in whatever you do.

The world is filled with people who look modest but are actually wealthy and people who appear rich but live on the edge of financial breakdown. Keep this in mind as you internalise your needs and set your goals. Financial freedom is hardly a function of high income but your ability to focus on what is important to you and not worry about what others think of you.

Without clarity on your needs and desires, life becomes an endless journey to nowhere. You may somehow reach somewhere—and likely after exhausting much of your time, effort, and energy. I don't think anyone would consider that success or happiness. Confidence, while important, is no substitute for proper preparation and clarity.

Discovering yourself requires introspection, visualisation, and thoughtful analysis. It compels you to think deeply about your priorities and align everything in your life with what is important to you. These priorities become your solid foundation and the standard by which you measure your life. They will not mislead you or suggest shortcuts to achieve them. They cannot be destroyed by theft, fire, or other calamities, and they don't naturally expire.

While working on them, you will not be restricted by your circumstances or the actions of others, which often hinder people from achieving their goals. It will bring consistency, strength, and grace to your life. Life gains meaning when you pursue what truly matters to you. There is no other meaning to life.

Meditation is one of the most powerful methods to train your mind and aid in prioritising what truly matters to you. We will explore the theory and practice of meditation later in the book. Let us not go there now. Instead, I suggest a simple technique to help you get some quick wins.

Keep a log of all your activities, whether it's walking, playing a game, gardening, cooking, cleaning, driving, brainstorming, creating presentations, managing a team, training, marketing, sales, volunteering, or even reading this book. Record each activity discreetly, and indicate whether your level of happiness while doing it is high or low. Maintain this log meticulously for three to four weeks. By doing so, you'll discern a pattern of activities that contribute to your happiness.

Continue with the activities that bring you happiness, and consider reducing, modifying, or delegating those that don't contribute to your happiness. If there are things you love to do that aren't already on your list, find ways to integrate them into your daily life—whether at home, work, or elsewhere—to double your happiness.

This approach will assist you in achieving balance and effectively allocating your attention to your work, health, family, friends, or societal engagement and will help prevent any one area from consuming you while others are neglected.

Most people don't know how unhappy they are. How their life could be different. They don't know how anything better is possible and what to ask for. They start believing they have the best possible situation or they no longer have a choice. They are designed by their subconscious mind to cope with their feelings about their unfulfilled needs and neglected desires, leading them to pretend to be happy. When you don't know what to do with your life, it means you don't know who you are.

Your life is measured by your results, not by your intentions. There is no measure of intent but whether you did it or not. If you didn't do something, it simply means you prioritised something else over it. Your excuses may serve as coping mechanisms to avoid the discomfort of unmet goals, but they also prevent you from seizing opportunities for growth and change.

When clarity is lacking, you might perceive yourself as acting out of compulsion even when that isn't the reality. This misunderstanding can lead to feelings of fear, anxiety, worry, arrogance, addiction, or boredom. Even experiencing just one of these emotions can reduce your happiness, while a combination of them can make you miserable. It doesn't stop there. You'll behave poorly toward yourself and others, inadvertently hurting your loved ones and those who matter most to you.

One day, a farmer was lying on his coir-woven couch, enjoying the evening sun in his farmhouse courtyard. His shining red tractor, parked on the other side of the courtyard, made it picture-perfect.

His wife was preparing tea and snacks for everyone at home as the children had just returned from school. Meanwhile, the children were busy watering their flowering and vegetable gardens around the house.

Usually, his wife would bring tea and snacks to the courtyard, and the family would gather to enjoy them. It was a time for sharing stories from the children's day at school.

The farmer would head to the farm with a small team of workers early in the morning, returning home by lunchtime. After a day's work, he was now relaxing and enjoying the warmth of the evening sun.

At that moment, a businessman passed by the farmer's house. He was staying at a nearby homestay, taking a week-long break after a busy year of work. He was busy talking on the phone when he noticed the farmer sitting leisurely on the couch.

'Hey, young man, don't you have work to do?' the businessman asked.

'I am done for the day,' replied the farmer with a charming smile.

As he often did with his team, the businessman felt compelled to motivate the farmer to be more productive.

'You should be working instead of lounging on the couch,' he advised.

The farmer, taken aback, smiled, ran his fingers over his beard, and asked.

'And what would happen if I did, sir?'

'Well, you could increase production and earn more money,' suggested the businessman.

'And then?' asked the farmer, maintaining his smile.

The businessman responded. 'You can buy or lease more land, deploy a much bigger team, produce huge quantities, earn a lot of money—and the best part is your people will do all the work for you!'

'And then what will I get, sir?' the farmer asked once more. The businessman, surprised and slightly irritated, reluctantly answered.

'You can become so rich that you will never have to work hard again. You can spend the rest of your days sitting at home, relaxed, after a moderate work day and enjoy your time with your family.'

The farmer continued to smile and replied, 'And what do you think I am doing right now, sir?'

Only when you don't know yourself, do other people's opinions become important.

From childhood, we're conditioned to seek association and validation, though every human being is a fully fledged individual with boundless potential and possibilities. We're often defined by family names, parents' professions, educational qualifications, affiliations with groups, and workplaces. If you know who you are and what is important to you, you may no longer need such validations.

No person is inherently superior to another. The only difference lies in the extent of their efforts despite challenges. Factors such as family background, religion, geographic location, education, profession, affiliations, gender, or sexual orientation don't define who you truly are. They are your own creations, illusions, and perceptions.

What truly matters is how you utilise your body and mind to achieve what's most meaningful to you and live joyfully.

I call it 'JoyLiv.' Let it become your true identity—and let Joyful Living be your real validation.

The real you!

Let us focus only on that!

Step 2

Master Your Mind

Your mind controls your body, so it is crucial that you master your mind. Either you master your mind or it masters you.

Let us delve into the second critical component of you: your mind—the place where everything in your life first unfolds.

Where is your mind located?

Some may point to their chest or forehead when referring to the mind. But is it truly located there?

Not exactly.

Your mind is present throughout your entire body.

As you know, your mind begins with a neural network and memory, and continues to develop as your beliefs, likes, dislikes, and indifferences, all influenced by your life experiences.

What is an experience? It's the thoughts and feelings associated with people, life forms, places, or things, during a specific time frame.

All your reactions and responses to anything—living or non-living—depend solely on your mind. You cannot see the real world as it is—only as it is interpreted by your mind. Your mind serves as your sole source of reference and is essential for your continuity and survival, much like how a computer's hardware cannot operate without its software.

It was many years ago when a friend of mine, who lives abroad, came to India for holiday. During their visit, they came to our home, and, after lunch, we went out together in my car.

As we were driving, we came across a black cow walking down the road. I carefully overtook it in the adjacent lane, just as I would any other vehicle. As you may know, in many parts of India, roads are shared not only by vehicles but also by animals, which, in their own way, seem to follow traffic rules—even stopping at traffic lights to avoid speeding vehicles!

Just then, my friend's seven-year-old son saw the cow through the car window and started shouting, 'Elephant! Elephant!'

My daughter, who was about the same age, quickly corrected him: 'Ayye, that's a cow, not an elephant!'

Having grown up abroad, he had not seen enough cows and elephants to distinguish accurately between a black cow and an elephant. This is how our life experiences shape our minds and our understanding of the world around us.

How the Mind Works

Let's understand how your mind functions—how it interprets and responds to everything you encounter—so that we can explore ways to maximise its potential.

Your body's five senses—eyes, ears, nose, tongue, and skin—manage the initial stage of perception. They convert physical stimuli from your environment into electrical signals or chemical reactions within your body, initiating information processing.

In subsequent stages, your body's neural network generates physical sensations in response to environmental stimuli, allowing you to experience them. Your likes, dislikes, or indifferences to what you see, hear, smell, taste, or touch manifest as various combinations of bodily sensations. Without associated physical sensations in your body, you wouldn't perceive or find relevance in them. For you, physical sensations represent the only reality; there is no such thing as a mental reality.

For example, consider someone calling you 'silly.'

First, in the cognition phase, your ears, as sense organs, convert the spoken word's sound waves into electrical signals when they reach them.

In the second part, in the recognition phase, a specific region of your brain receives these signals and uses them to interpret what you have heard. If English is not your language, it holds no meaning for you, and that's the end of the matter. Obviously, you can understand what is said only if you have learnt English, and the meaning of the word 'silly' will be the same for all those who know the English language.

The third stage is most crucial. In this reaction phase, your mind evaluates details such as who said it, the tone, whether it was said in public or private, and whether it occurred in front of your friend, spouse, boss, or subordinate—all based on how your memory has stored the information. Depending on your life experiences, you might have a different response for each scenario.

If it was said in private, you might not care; if it was said in public, you might feel embarrassed about it; and if it was said in front of your subordinates, you might even become angry—All in response to the same word.

Once your mind finds a matching scenario, in the fourth stage—or sensation phase—your neural network commands your body to produce sensations, which represent your feelings about the exact situation in which you heard the word. Although the word, its translation into electrical signals, and its interpretation as 'silly' remain the same, your reactions, bodily sensations, and feelings may differ depending on the context, and vary from anyone else's.

It's all within you. They depend solely on the specific instructions stored in your memory and are based on the experiences you had in life, referred to as your mental conditioning, beliefs, or personality. You made it yourself.

You describe a certain food as spicy, bland, good, or bad. It's not the inherent quality of the food itself, but rather the sensations it evokes on your mouth and the opinions you've stored about it in your memory. That's why a dish you love might be disliked by someone else. Similarly, you might grow to love a food you initially disliked. All your reactions to what you hear, see, touch, smell, or taste change and evolve within you over time.

Imagine a scenario where someone strikes you in the face out of anger versus another where they do it to kill a mosquito that bit you on the face. Although the latter might cause more physical pain, you might be more accepting of it.

No one can disrespect or hurt you unless you allow it in your mind. Your happiness or misery always stems from within, not from external sources.

Things or situations themselves have no inherent nature. Your experience with them could evoke happiness or sadness. The quality of you is not defined by external circumstances or others' behaviour, but by what is within you regarding them.

Your actions are largely guided by your personal beliefs, such as 'Anand will step up because of his positive attitude,' 'that political party will or won't follow through,' 'she can prepare a simple meal even when unwell,' 'he can manage it despite being busy,' 'he's lazy and won't finish it,' 'he deserves his current situation because of how he treated Preethi,' and many more.

These beliefs, shaped by your life experiences and unique to yourself, often lead to a self-perception that differs from how others see you.

Your reactions and feelings towards anything or anyone will intensify if you hold strong preferences for them. For many people, these preferences often indicate deeper issues they struggle to confront.

For instance, if they feel inadequate compared to someone else's success, they may seek reasons to feel better and cope with the situation—like 'students who excel academically won't be well-rounded,' 'hard work compromises family life,' 'money breeds arrogance,' or 'career growth requires sacrificing individuality.' While such beliefs may offer temporary comfort, they can also become significant barriers to progress.

Although your nose is right above your mouth, you may not notice if your mouth smells bad, but others will. Will they tell you about it, or just politely keep their distance?

Recognising your own shortcomings requires heightened sensitivity and observation. Being aware of your mental conditioning, willing to examine it, testing it against reality, and being open to change are all hallmarks of conscious living. Failing to do so will burden you with life experiences meant for growth and ease, hindering your ability to progress.

A Guru and his disciple were journeying from their hermitage to a nearby village. The path led them through a dense forest, with a river to cross.

Upon reaching the riverbank, they encountered a young woman, visibly anxious about crossing due to the strong flow and undercurrents. The Guru sensed her distress, lifted her, and carried her across the river upon his shoulders. Once they safely reached the other side, he respectfully set her down, bowed to her, and resumed walking.

Some time later, the disciple pondered the incident and eventually approached the Guru with a question.

'We are sannyasis. Is it appropriate for us to carry a young woman, especially upon our shoulders?'

The Guru replied, 'I left her at the riverbank a long time ago. It seems you're still carrying her.'

Your identity is shaped by what resides in your mind. Acting with integrity beyond your beliefs is nearly impossible. Forcing yourself to do so will result in artificiality and inconsistency. It will disturb your comfort, clarity, and sense of control, leading to confusion, stress, and unhappiness.

This is why change is always difficult.

Even though your thoughts arise from within rather than from external stimuli, they operate similarly. Your body's physical sensations are also produced by your neural network in response to these thoughts, generating feelings. This is how you respond to particular thoughts.

Even years later, the 'silly' incident can still evoke feelings whenever you recall it, depending on your reactions to them stored in your memory. You even respond to it in your dreams, as your subconscious continues to process them.

Your neural network and memory can change over time as a result of both conscious and unconscious changes, leading to shifts in reactions, bodily sensations, and emotions. Training your mind involves consciously altering your neural pathways to influence how you respond to particular situations or thoughts.

The mind controls the body, so it is vital to master the mind. Either you master the mind or it masters you!

Training Your Mind

When you're in good health, your body's physical thermostat maintains a constant temperature of 98.6 degrees Fahrenheit, ensuring proper bodily function. Your body retains this warmth regardless of external conditions such as heat, cold, wind, or rain. To eliminate bacteria or viruses that have entered your body, your temperature increases slightly, which we commonly call a fever. You know how draining a fever can be until your body returns to its normal temperature.

It's remarkable that all these functions are fully automatic. If you had to manage them manually, you would have gone mad long ago, and your body would have collapsed. Similarly, to control your responses to various occurrences around you, your mind must maintain an 'emotional thermostat' to prevent them from draining you.

In the past, people were generally at ease, but nowadays, most of us are constantly occupied with phones, computers, television and social media—keeping the mind perpetually busy processing both physical stimuli and thoughts. Interestingly, your nervous system uses more energy than any other part of your body. In fact, a busy mind can drain more energy than physical labour, often leaving you exhausted.

On average, a person has thousands of thoughts each day, with about 90 percent of them being the same as the previous day's. Most of these are repetitive, often dwelling on the past or worrying about the future, fueling negative emotions and keeping us from fully living in the present. Interestingly, if you observe closely, more than 90 percent of the things we worry about never actually happen.

Your thoughts are conscious or subconscious creations of your own mind. They can consume you if you engage with them, but if you withdraw your attention, they often fade away. I'm not suggesting you stop thinking altogether, but rather that you learn to choose one thought over another.

One of the simplest ways to regulate your thoughts is by observing your inhalation and exhalation. As you start observing your breath, you become conscious of your thoughts. If a thought proves useful, you may continue because the intention isn't to stop thinking altogether. However, if it's not useful, you can discard it and move on. Try it now to see how it works.

Initially, you may realise that more than 90 percent of your thoughts are unproductive. However, as you learn the art of observing your breath and thoughts, you'll begin to spend your time and effort only on useful thoughts. This will conserve your energy and enhance your efficiency, effectiveness, tranquillity, and happiness. Keep practicing because this is an important aspect of meditation, which we will explore soon.

We all face problems. However, worrying won't improve our situation; it will only diminish our ability to deal with them effectively. Simply saying 'Don't worry' might sound like a cliché and won't really help. Instead, observe the situation and respond appropriately in the following scenarios.

Scenario 1:

Although you're facing a challenge, you're in an advantageous position if you know how to address it. Take initiative and work towards resolving it. Once you've done your best to find a solution, stop dwelling on it.

Is it helpful to dwell on, 'I should have done it sooner?' No, because there's nothing you can do about it now. Although each problem is unique, there may be value in taking some time to reflect on what improvements might be made in the future.

Scenario 2:

If there's nothing you can do about a situation right now, the wisest approach is to wait for it to pass—and sooner or later, it surely does. For example, being stuck in traffic due to an accident, waiting for your flight to take off because of bad weather, or awaiting a diagnosis or recovering from an illness.

As you overcome worry, you will exude confidence. No one is born with confidence; it is developed over time.

What does a 'trained mind' mean?

Let's take the example of anger. If you observe closely, it typically unfolds in four phases. First, you begin to feel anger building. Then, you experience the anger, hold onto it, and eventually, it fades away.

Though anger is a natural and potent emotion, it often results in remorse. By the time your anger subsides, most of the damage has already been done. If no one has the courage to tell you later, you might not even be aware of how angry you were.

Anger is a sharp weapon that can overshadow all your goodness and accomplishments, while also causing lasting wounds in others. People may forget what you have done for them, but they won't forget how you made them feel.

Feeling anger is a good example of momentarily losing mental equilibrium for a while and then returning to a normal state. If you're unable to return, you may be seen as insane. That's why there's often just a thin line between being considered sane or insane. How often you breach this boundary determines the nature of your life and how it impacts those around you.

There's a trace of madness in everyone—but when it exceeds socially acceptable limits, it becomes a problem for others. To make matters worse, the person crossing the line often sees their behaviour as completely normal from their own perspective.

With a trained mind, you can recognise when you're about to become angry, are angry, or remain angry, and take steps to reverse it. This ability enables you to express anger appropriately without inflicting harm on yourself or others. In fact, controlled anger can be an effective tool to set boundaries if it's the most fitting emotional response for the situation. And this applies not only to anger, but also to other emotions.

In the farmland of a village, there lived a magnificent snake known for its aggressive behaviour. Whenever it felt threatened, the snake would bite the villagers, striking fear into them. Tragically, the snake's bites had led to fatalities among men, women, and children, prompting villagers to abandon their farms, thereby affecting their livelihood.

Concerned about the situation, the villagers sought help from the village wise man. Recognising the seriousness of the issue, he chose to confront the snake.

The wise man helped the snake to understand the consequences of its actions and persuaded it to stop biting people. With the snake's change in behaviour, the villagers began cautiously to return to their farms. However, they continued to chase and throw stones at the snake, despite its restraint.

As time passed, the snake suffered serious injuries from the villagers' attacks. Recognising its plight, the snake sought advice and help from the wise man, expressing concern that the villagers were now chasing it everywhere and were no longer afraid of it.

The wise man, disappointed by the pitiful situation of the once-privileged snake, questioned, 'I urged you not to bite anyone to spare their lives, but why did you even stop hissing?'

The human mind tends to react more strongly to negative events than to equally positive ones. This is because it's wired to detect and respond to threats, violations, and failures. As a result, good stories are often only one-tenth as common as bad ones.

Familiarity with people can breed contempt, leading to disregard and disrespect. Gossip, which usually centres on the moral or social missteps of others, is often negative and often inaccurate. Even in financial matters, the pain of loss often outweighs the joy of an equivalent gain.

Staying positive is not natural—it requires training your mind to be so. Children rarely complain, whether it's about the weather, food, school, friends, or anything else. But as you grow older, you start complaining more. Seeing the beauty in the things you have and the world around you can be difficult when you are unhappy, which further deepens your unhappiness.

The good news is: you can reverse this tendency. And it's essential that you do.

When you speak or act positively, your mind uplifts your spirits and reduces your tendency toward negativity. The opposite is equally true. Find positives in everything and everyone, even if you notice the negatives. Appreciate people for their appearance, thoughts, ideas, and actions. This helps you significantly reduce and narrow down their drawbacks to only those that truly deserve your concern.

When it comes to gossip, speak about others as if they were present and listening, and only share information that is both true and useful to those hearing it.

Consciously avoid dull, draining phrases like 'bad weather,' 'very busy,' 'no use,' 'not well,' 'tired,' or 'hopeless.' When you use such words, you not only convey negativity to others but also feel it yourself. Instead, choose bright, cheerful words like 'good news,' 'great opportunity,' 'sweet spot,' 'going great,' 'wonderful,' 'brilliant,' or 'fantastic'—to lift your mood and those around you.

Infuse positivity into everything you say.

Instead of saying, 'The day was horrible; my vehicle broke down at the wrong time,' say, 'Luckily, I found a taxi right away when my vehicle broke down and still made it on time.' Likewise, rather than saying, 'It's tough to win,' try, 'The competition is strong, but we have some advantages.' Of course, with genuineness and enthusiasm.

Optimism isn't about believing everything will be perfect—that's complacency. True optimism is the belief that the end outcome will be good, even when there are setbacks along the way.

Negative emotions are a part of life, but it's crucial to consciously consider what might be constructive at that moment and react accordingly. Being positive is a great skill. Train your mind to envision beyond what it is today to what it can be. Walk faster, speak up, smile broadly, and laugh freely.

Maintaining a sense of humor and finding moments of laughter is essential. Smiling and laughing trigger the release of mood-lifting chemicals in your body that help break the cycle of negativity, ease anxiety, and boost your positivity even more.

Reflect on one action you're currently not doing, but if you start, it could bring a significant positive change to your life and to those around you. Make a sincere commitment to include it in your life from today. And don't stop there—think about what the next one could be.

Positivity amplifies your ability and potential to achieve anything in life. Negativity, on the other hand, is like a flat tire—you won't get far unless you change it.

Dance whenever you get the chance. There are no rules to casual dancing—just let the music take over and move in any way that makes you happy. Don't worry about what others might think. Deep down, they'd love to join you, but their own inhibitions hold them back. The more carefree and playful you are, the more you'll benefit—and the more fun they'll have watching you. After all, bringing joy to others while having fun yourself is a privilege, isn't it?

It reminds me of an inspiring story.

In a hospital, there were two patients sharing a twin room, both bedridden. One patient had a bed near the window, while the other had a view of only a plain wall. However, the patient next to the window used to describe everything outside to the other patient.

'The birds are building their nest, squirrels squabble over a ripe mango, and a kingfisher waits patiently on a nearby tree, gazing at the pond below,' he would say. 'Today, there are four water lilies in the pond, with many butterflies fluttering around,' and many such scenes.

Despite his pain and weakness, the patient by the window would frequently look out of the window, vividly describing the beautiful views to his companion.

A few days later, the patient by the window passed away. The other patient asked the nurse if he could be moved to the window bed. The nurse, though surprised by the request, agreed. Eagerly, the patient looked out through the window, only to find nothing but empty, barren ground in his view.

'What happened to the trees, birds, pond, water lilies?' he asked.

'They were never there,' she replied.

He said, 'The other patient used to describe them when he looked out the window.'

The nurse replied, 'He was an amazing person. Perhaps he simply wanted to encourage you.'

Mindfulness

Mindfulness is a powerful method to clear your mind and fully enjoy each moment. The goal is to stay aware of the present without getting caught up in the past or worrying about the future. When you're mindful, you become an observer of everything happening within and around you—as if someone else is doing it and you're simply watching.

Observe your posture and every movement of your body at all times—whether it's your hands, legs, head, or any other part. This will help you eliminate unnecessary physical movements, such as running your fingers through your beard or mustache, adjusting hair that falls across your face, shaking your leg, or frequently touching your nose, lips or any other body part.

By keeping your body still, you can calm your mind, increase your awareness, choose deliberate movements rather than compulsive ones, and bring ease and grace into your presence.

Similarly, observe your thoughts, speech, and feelings at all times. This will help you halt or manage them better—as discussed previously regarding anger. We will explore techniques to achieve this more easily in the section on Meditation.

When it comes to everyday activities—such as cooking—pay attention to how the texture, colour and aroma of each ingredient change as it cooks. This mindful focus not only quiets wandering thoughts but also draws you fully into the task at hand. Your engagement and attention to detail will also ensure the dish turns out well. You can apply the same approach to washing utensils or any other daily task.

During your bath, focus on the sensations of water flowing over your body, the scent of soap, the feeling of your head becoming wet, and so on. Without awareness, you may even find yourself wondering whether you washed your face with soap after the bath—does this sound familiar?

While walking, running, or exercising, pay attention to your steps, body movements, breath, sensations and the wind touching your face. This mindful approach can help you moderate your activities and make them more enjoyable.

Observe all that is happening around you and appreciate the beauty of the rain, leaves, flowers, fruits and traffic, and anything else. Avoid distractions like listening to music, watching videos, or observing others. This will help you stay present, be with yourself, and enjoy the power of now. This is how the most beautiful moments of excitement, happiness or joy occur in your life—not by simply thinking about them.

Once you become comfortable with it, you'll be able to engage in simple multitasking—like thinking through a project outline, preparing a presentation, drafting an article, or planning a talk—all while staying present. This doubles the use of your time and enhances productivity.

You can clear your mind by reciting *Mantras*. In Sanskrit, '*Man*' means mind, and '*tra*' means tool. *Mantras* are collections of words arranged in specific patterns and recited to particular tunes. These patterns and rhythms are structured for easy, continuous repetition without fatigue, helping to free your mind from wandering thoughts.

Some words may not carry literal meanings but are chosen for the positive vibrations they produce in your body and surroundings, benefiting you and others. It's the simplest method to calm the mind, often practiced by those with religious beliefs.

Your hobbies can also help to clear your mind. But what is a hobby?

It's anything undertaken willingly and without compulsion—like gardening, cooking, singing, dancing, painting, playing a musical instrument or a game. You might spend time with people you don't care about, do things you don't want to do, eat food you dislike, or even share a bed with someone reluctantly—but you can't approach a hobby that way. Hobbies fully engage you, harmonising your mind and body without mental distractions, allowing you to experience joy.

Even if it's your regular work and you're doing it willingly, loving what you do (LoWyD) can make it feel as though it were a hobby. It becomes seamless—no one can tell if you're working or playing. You might not even feel the need to take a break or seek entertainment elsewhere like going to a movie, party, or watching television. Those small distractions may lose their significance in your life.

Meditation

We've kept this topic on hold for some time now—thank you for your patience.

One of the most effective approaches for clearing your mind, training it, and relaxing your body is meditation.

Meditation isn't just an act but through maintaining your body and mind in a specific way, you naturally enter a meditative state.

What distinguishes meditation from sleep?

During meditation, your mind remains conscious with fewer or no thoughts, while your body remains at complete rest. A similar experience can happen as you're about to fall asleep, although this is usually short-lived before you drift into sleep.

During sleep, your body rests, but the key difference is that you're not conscious.

Physically resting while remaining aware is the best way to clear your mind and relax your body. However, as many find maintaining awareness challenging, sleep often becomes the preferred alternative. Yet, achieving a relaxed and rejuvenated state through sleep takes longer than meditation. That's why just fifteen to twenty minutes of meditation can be as restorative as two hours of sleep.

During meditation, your brainwaves shift from their usual frequencies to a tranquil state, leading to the release of mood-elevating chemicals in your body.

Though your eyes are essential for perceiving the world around you, they can also be a major source of distraction and consume considerable energy. Therefore, it's advisable to keep your eyes closed during meditation and even during other activities when they don't need to be open.

Solitude, stillness and silence will enable you to distinctly connect with the three essential aspects of yourself—your body, mind, and YOU.

During meditation, you consciously observe your thoughts or bodily sensations without getting involved in them. Although these involve different techniques, they yield similar outcomes because they are interrelated, as your thoughts generate bodily sensations.

This practice trains your mind by dissolving neural pathways that aren't important to you and strengthening those that matter more—something that's difficult to achieve through any other method. In fact, any Artificial Intelligence (AI) software is modelled on similar principles, discarding paths that lead to undesired outcomes while reinforcing those that lead to desired ones.

This process will help you re-evaluate your beliefs and view yourself as just another life on the planet, rather than identifying yourself as a male or female, Black or White, Indian or American, Hindu or Christian, Socialist or Communist, or anything else.

It will diminish your inhibitions, fear of failure and fear of death. Consequently, your thoughts will decrease, and possibilities will broaden.

As your thoughts, reactions to them, and bodily sensations decrease, your overall bodily reverberations also diminish. If you are highly action-oriented and have low consciousness, your body reverberations may measure around 15. Such heightened bodily reactions often dull various sensibilities and sensitivities. This applies to over 90 percent of people, posing a considerable barrier to sensing, feeling, observing, introspecting, and visualising many aspects of your surroundings or yourself.

When bodily reverberations decrease to twelve, you can feel not only yourself but also others and even animals, and at a level of 9, you can feel the plants. When it decreases to 6, you become attuned to subtle energies surrounding you, and at 3, you can perceive the vastness of the universe.

This is how spiritual gurus have utilised their bodies to sense and their minds to perceive, deciphering the functioning of the body, mind, cosmos, and the mysteries of life. Don't view these numbers as absolute measures but rather as a relative scale of consciousness and its impact on you.

Let us now explore both techniques—observing thoughts and bodily sensations in meditation—in detail to help you practise them.

Observing Thoughts

This technique involves observing your thoughts without engaging with them. They may arise and pass without drawing your focus, and over time, their frequency will reduce. With regular practice, you may notice that thoughts become infrequent during your sessions and even after.

If a thought troubles you, you can shift your attention to your breath for a few cycles, as we discussed, to help ease the distraction.

By following the steps outlined below, this meditation technique becomes straightforward and easy to practise, allowing you to practise it anywhere.

1. It becomes easier when you're slightly fatigued and mildly hungry. Therefore, just before lunch and dinner are the most suitable times to meditate. Practise it at both times and no more.

2. Sit with your back well supported, either on a chair with a backrest or on the floor leaning against a wall. Cross your right ankle over your left (remove your shoes and socks to allow skin contact) and place your right palm over your left palm, facing upward in your lap. Keep your head relaxed and upright. See the illustrations below.

3. Note the time and close your eyes. Begin the meditation without any expectations and refrain from liking or disliking any specific thought, emotion, or outcome. Don't react to anything until the meditation is complete.

4. Observe your breath for two to three cycles (one inhalation and one exhalation is one cycle). Do not give in to your thoughts or resist them. If a thought persists, refocus on your breath for two to three cycles to help alleviate the distraction.

5. After twelve to twenty minutes, you will naturally reach the end of your meditation, feeling refreshed and disinclined to continue. Open your eyes and check the time again. If less than twelve minutes have passed, close your eyes and continue until fifteen to twenty minutes have elapsed since your initial time check.

Meditation posture: Legs crossed

Meditation posture: Legs stretched

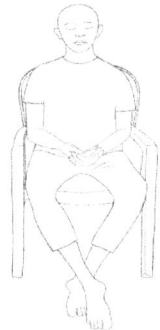

Meditation posture: Sitting on the chair

If you meditate at the same time every day, your body will naturally prompt you to meditate around that time. Similar to how you feel sleepy around your usual bedtime, and experience the best sleep in your usual sleeping place, meditating at a consistent time and place promotes deeper meditation. However, if you need to travel or work in different places, meditate wherever you can.

Ensure that the environment is conducive to meditation—neither too uncomfortable nor distracting. Avoid extremes in temperature, strong winds, excessive noise, unpleasant odours, and other distractions that could divert your attention.

Observing Body Sensations

This is the opposite of watching your thoughts. Instead, you focus on your body's sensations. As you know, every physical sensation you experience is your mind's response to a particular thought or external stimulus.

Using this technique, you gradually shift your focus from your head to your toes, scanning the entire body with fine detail—roughly one square inch at a time—paying close attention to every minor sensation in the area of focus.

By ignoring the corresponding sensations, you will gradually train your neural network to stop producing sensations for many of your thoughts. This technique can also reduce reactions to your thoughts at the subconscious level.

This is *Vipassana* meditation, one of the greatest teachings of Buddha. *Vipassana* means 'to see things as they really are.' To utilise this technique, you must practise observing even the smallest bodily sensations. However, this description alone may not be sufficient for you to practise the technique effectively, unlike the observing your thoughts technique.

I advise you to seek out a qualified *Vipassana* meditation teacher who can assist you in learning the practice. Anyone interested in learning it can receive support for free from *Vipassana* meditation centres worldwide.

Healthy Mind

A trained mind helps you manage your thoughts and reactions effectively. It fosters a positive outlook and sharpens your ability to observe, analyse, and introspect. It also supports you in discovering who you are, understanding what truly matters to you, visualising your goals, and using your whole brain—not just the dominant left or right side—to achieve them.

As you may know, the left side of your brain tends to function more logically and verbally, enabling you to think sequentially, break concepts down into smaller parts, analyse them, and articulate them in words.

In contrast, the right side of your brain is more intuitive and creative, enabling you to think holistically, recognise patterns and connections, and form mental images. Sadly, this aspect is often undervalued in a left-brain-dominated world that emphasises logic, measurement, and verbal communication. As a result, many people struggle to tap into their right-brain abilities—perhaps even you—until life's setbacks push them to seek innovative solutions for survival.

A trained mind will enable you to vividly visualize your needs and desires as images in your mind. Whether it's your home, clothes, car, partner, work, career, hobby, ideas, making a presentation, performance, or even cooking a dish—visualisation helps you form a clear picture of what you want, including how it will look and feel. The clearer you are, the higher your chances of achieving them efficiently.

Every accomplished individual—whether in work, the arts, sports, or any other field—clearly envisions, feels, and experiences their goals before taking action. Everything created by humans—from the clothes you wear, the chair you sit on, and the pen you use to write with to the very book you're reading now—existed in someone's mind before becoming reality.

While your creative right brain fosters clarity, your left brain plays a crucial role in organising the right brain's ideas into components, words, and plans, making them actionable. By using your whole brain to pursue your goals, you significantly enhance your ability to achieve them more effectively. Visualisation is essential for excelling in any endeavor.

A trained mind sharpens your clarity and awareness, boosting creativity, communication, relationships, and productivity, while reducing anger, anxiety and fear. Strong preferences regarding people, places, food, work, politics, religion, or anything else will gradually fade. Your comfort zones will loosen, offering more choices and opportunities you might not have noticed otherwise.

You'll begin living less reactively and compulsively, with a growing sense of grace. You may feel as though you're losing yourself, but in reality, you're reclaiming your authentic self and your true life.

Don't hold back—carry on!

Step 3

Health First

Even if you have everything else in life, you'll eventually realise that you have nothing without your health. Take very good care of it so you don't have to worry about it.

Whether they are your needs or desires, once you've gained clarity on them, you must put in the effort to make them a reality—they still exist only in your mind.

Everything happens twice in life: first in your mind, then in the real world.

To bring them to life, you've been gifted with the most sophisticated machine on the planet—your body. Of course, you must maintain it in excellent working condition for it to function efficiently and support you fully.

You may have noticed that even a basic device you purchase will have a detailed user manual. It explains how to set it up and use it, the optimal energy source for its best performance, how to protect it from the environment around it, necessary maintenance to prevent breakdowns, self-checks, diagnostics, and more.

Where's the instruction manual for the most complex machine on Earth—your body? How can you expect it to function well for long if you don't even know the basics of how it works?

It was a long-awaited trek to the Himalayas.

Our group comprised over twenty people, ranging in age from twenty-one to fifty-five. Preparations had been underway for more than six months under the guidance of a tour operator. Each of us had to submit a comprehensive health check-up report to their doctor for verification, and the trip was confirmed only upon the doctor's approval. Naturally, a few individuals couldn't get confirmation due to their health issues.

Finally, we were all set to go. Waterproof bags, jackets, raincoats, thermalwear, trekking shoes, and more—we had everything prepared. We flew in from different places and landed in Delhi by noon. In the afternoon, we travelled by minibus and reached the foothills of the magnificent and enchanting Himalayas by late evening. We camped there overnight, ready to start the trek the next day.

It was around sixteen kilometres of climb to a height of 3,500 metres. We began around 9 a.m. with the expectation of reaching the top by 4–5 p.m. The rain persisted throughout the trek. Occasionally, the bright hot sun would peep through for a couple of minutes, giving us hope that the rain was over, only for it to start pouring again soon after—the typical Himalayan weather.

The temperature hovered below zero degrees Celsius, and the wind made it even colder. Once we crossed the halfway mark, the lack of oxygen to breathe started adding to the existing challenges.

Many of us were climbing alone, each at their own pace. Some reached the top around 4 PM, while others trickled in until late evening. Everyone got drenched in the rain, and most of our belongings were soaked.

There was no heating or hot water at our accommodation on top. Most people were exhausted and collapsed into bed, crying out for help due to muscle cramps. I suggested some stretching exercises to relieve their pain, but they were unable to even sit up or stand. For some, this realisation of limited amenities led to emotional breakdowns.

A few of us ventured out, gathering firewood from local villagers to keep warm until midnight. However, others missed out on the warmth and the simple dal-rice dinner arranged for us.

Very few people were able to walk down the next day, even though it was much easier than the climb. They had to be carried by local people as a paid service. I felt sorry for both of them. While they were being transported, the rest of us went around shopping and waited for them at the foothills.

I vividly remember one of them saying when they were brought to the vehicle, 'Hey friends, please collect the dead bodies and place them in our seats.'

We had many more places to explore in the Himalayas in the following days. Those individuals mostly remained in the vehicle as it was challenging for them to get in and out. The pain, frustration, and embarrassment were evident from their expressions and their words. It seemed they had everything in their lives except physical fitness.

Your physical health is largely influenced by the food you eat, the exercise you do, and the rest you get—mental and physical.

However, maintaining good health is increasingly challenging in today's world. Poor air quality, contaminated water, pesticide residue in food, and low nutritional value of the diet contribute to this difficulty. Additionally, the lack of physical exercise, driven by increasing comfort and convenience, along with the mental stress from modern lifestyles, further compounds the issue.

In the past, people seldom experienced stress, and when they did, it was typically in life-threatening situations. Today, individuals often feel anxious and frustrated due to the high expectations at work, home, and beyond. Moreover, the constant bombardment of social media, emails, and instant messages adds to their stress and anxiety. This impairs concentration, slows cognitive processing, and increases errors, and further fuels stress and various health issues.

Diseases

Every life on the planet, including humans, should be in a state of ease to function well. When this ease is lost, we refer to it as disease.

When your body is kept in good condition, it has the best defence mechanisms to combat invasive bacteria, viruses or other ailments and restore ease to you. However, your body must fight these battles on its own.

Nobody else can endure your illness for you, not even your closest loved ones. You cannot share it with someone beyond just talking about it. In fact, discussing your illness with others often results in dull conversations for them. Moreover, the more you talk about it, the worse it tends to get for you, even for something as simple as a cold or a fever.

As you may have noticed, even after a few hours of continuous physical activity, you might not feel completely exhausted. But a mild fever can leave you drained—unable to move or even stand. This shows how much effort and energy your body uses to defend itself against intruders like bacteria or viruses. If your body can't spend that kind of energy, you'll likely fall ill, and it may take a while for you to recover.

Ayurveda—a natural system of medicine, originated in India thousands of years ago and is renowned for its holistic approach to physical and mental health. In Sanskrit, '*Ayur*' means life and '*veda*' means knowledge, translating to 'knowledge of life.'

Ayurveda places significant emphasis on prevention and views any ailment as a manifestation of toxins in the body. Its treatments are aimed at removing these toxins and implementing lifestyle interventions to address their root cause. Therapies include herbal medicines, special diets, yoga, medical oils, massage and surgical techniques.

Conditions like diabetes, hypertension, raised cholesterol, and related disorders of vital organs such as the heart, liver, and kidneys are largely driven by lifestyle choices. In the past, these typically appeared in people in their fifties or sixties, but now they're increasingly common among those in their twenties and thirties.

The good news is that if you haven't developed these conditions yet, you can take proactive steps to prevent them. And even if they're already present, changes in your diet and way of life can help you manage them—and in many cases, reduce or even eliminate the need for medication.

A patient visited the doctor complaining of headaches, chest pain, and stomach issues that had been troubling him for some time.

The doctor diagnosed the patient with high blood pressure, high cholesterol, and a couple of other associated complications. Upon detailed inquiry into the patient's dietary and lifestyle habits, the doctor found that nothing was in order.

The doctor advised the patient, 'You must eat on time, avoid deep-fried items, junk food, carbonated beverages, and alcohol. Ensure you get adequate sleep and don't miss your brisk morning walk.'

The doctor recommended a specific dietary plan for the patient, suggesting:

Breakfast: A medium-sized bowl of cereal with half a cup of milk.

Lunch: A small bowl of rice with a medium-sized bowl of pulses and vegetables..

Evening Snack: A medium-sized bowl of cut fruits.

Dinner: A medium-sized bowl of green salad and one or two slices of bread.

The patient appeared happy with the dietary recommendations, which surprised the doctor. The doctor reassured the patient, saying, 'That will suffice.'

The patient enthusiastically asked, 'Doctor, should I have them before or after my regular meal?'

A healthy diet, regular physical exercise, adequate sleep and a sound mind are your best medicine.

In certain special cases, such as infections, medicines may be necessary, and in some instances, surgical intervention to remove a troublesome organ or tissue may be required. However, these situations will be rare exceptions if you take good care of your body and mind.

Physical Fitness

Exercise is vital for physical fitness, as most people are aware. However, many still neglect it, often citing a lack of time as the main excuse.

Are you suggesting that you don't have time to maintain your most valuable asset, which ultimately enables you to pursue your life goals? I would encourage you to avoid making excuses when it comes to essentials in life. Instead, consider making changes within yourself.

Wake up slightly earlier. It's the first task of your day, and there's much more to accomplish before it ends. If you struggle with the first task itself, it can set the tone for the rest of your day.

I'm not downplaying the effort it takes to leave a warm bed for a cold room, especially to exert yourself physically. It might even feel like gravity is doubled at that hour, but if you persevere, your determination will grow stronger. Remember, your life won't change unless you change your daily routine.

If you genuinely lack time, you're the one who needs it most. Falling ill or injuring yourself could lead to lost days for yourself, your family, and dependents. It could also deplete some or all of your savings. Staying healthy means being more available, more productive and ultimately saving more time than you spend on exercise. Spending time on your health is time well spent.

Your childhood physical activities and agility contribute to good muscle strength and body flexibility. However, if you don't maintain these activities, they will begin to decline starting in your teenage years, and you'll lose them faster than you gained them.

This can lead to injuries if you engage in physical activities beyond your regular routine. Additional chores at home, participating in activities during office or family gatherings, a hike or long walk during a pilgrimage or even changing a flat tyre during a journey can unexpectedly strain your body and lead to injuries, spoiling your day(s).

Muscles are like a second heart, supporting blood circulation and contributing to the efficient and smooth functioning of your body. When they become weak, your heart must take on the additional load to compensate—but it can't sustain that strain for long, often leading to hypertension, metabolic disorders and cardiovascular issues.

If you become overweight, develop joint pain or experience other ailments, you may find it challenging to even begin physical exercises if they weren't already part of your routine. This can become a significant barrier to addressing your needs and desires, potentially affecting you for the remainder of your life. Let's make sure this doesn't happen to you.

When I worked in a government organisation, entry and exit times were strictly enforced. We had to clock in and clock out using our ID cards at the attendance kiosk near the gate. A grace period of three minutes was permitted, but beyond that, the system automatically deducted from our leave balance.

Despite being a large manufacturing facility for defense systems, I rarely encountered any fatal accidents during my tenure, thanks to the company's high safety standards and the presence of a fully equipped onsite hospital.

Ironically, there were incidents of people collapsing and even dying near the attendance kiosks while rushing to clock in when they were running late, even though their bodies were capable of running a marathon if they had maintained their health.

The good news is that staying fit doesn't require hours of exercise. Many people, including yourself, may be unaware of this. Engaging in any of the following activities five days a week at a moderate level is sufficient:

- Daily tasks such as cleaning, gardening, or other physical activities that exercise most parts of your body for at least two hours a day.

- Activities such as brisk walking, running, cycling, swimming, playing games, practicing yoga, gym workouts, or similar intensity exercises for one hour a day.

To assess your current muscle strength, I recommend performing a simple test. Try holding a plank position—refer to the illustration below. If you find it difficult or experience any discomfort, stop immediately.

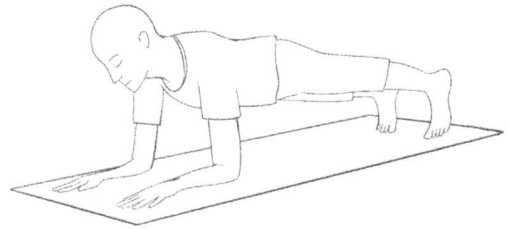

Muscle Strength Test

If you're unable to hold the plank position for two to three minutes, it indicates that your muscle strength requires improvement.

Start today with one of the exercises mentioned above and gradually progress to the recommended levels over three to six months. Rushing the process can lead to pain and injury, potentially causing you to give up.

Once you reach those levels, you can increase the duration or difficulty for added enjoyment or to further enhance your fitness—though the activities and levels mentioned above are sufficient to maintain your fitness and allow you to engage in what matters most in life. If you have any underlying medical conditions, it's essential to consult your doctor before starting any new exercise regimen.

Even with strong muscles, injuries can still occur due to a lack of body flexibility. While many of these activities can improve your flexibility, it's important to assess it as well. Why take chances with your most important asset?

Keep your back straight and your feet close together. Slowly bend forward without bending your knees, bringing the tips of your fingers to your toes—refer to the illustration below—and hold that position for four to five seconds.

If you're unable to touch your toes and hold the position for four to five seconds, it indicates that your body needs to work on its flexibility. Consider adding some basic stretching exercises to your routine. It's that simple.

Surya Namaskar is a simple yogic exercise that can enhance both strength and flexibility simultaneously. If you have any underlying medical conditions, speak with your doctor before you begin.

Body Flexibility Test

Performing the same exercises every day may not effectively engage or develop all your muscles, potentially leading to injuries if you deviate from your routine.

If you regularly walk or run, try varying your route by including uphill climbs, downhill stretches, roads and trails. Instead of sticking to just one activity, try to incorporate three to four different ones—like running, gym workouts, yoga, cleaning or gardening—throughout the week. This variety helps engage different muscle groups, strengthens your entire body and maintains flexibility.

Beyond strength, flexibility, and endurance, regular physical exercise offers a multitude of benefits. It helps eliminate toxins from your body, releases suppressed emotions, enhances optimism by reducing anger, anxiety and fear, boosts mental processing speed, improves focus, and increases your capacity for learning. What more could one ask for?

In the past, sports were a regular activity and community event aiming to combine play, exercise, and enjoyment for overall well-being and to strengthen relationships. Football, in particular, gained popularity because it doesn't require any equipment or gear; anyone can play it anywhere. However, the economic pursuit has lately commercialised sports to promote products and services rather than nurturing relationships and well-being.

Why did I advise you to exercise only five days per week and give your body rest on the other two days? Your muscles stretch during the exercise, causing tiny tears. If you give them a break, they join and come back stronger than before to protect you from injury.

Your emotional restraints also work the same way. Pushing beyond previous boundaries may cause tears in your emotional muscles, but they mend stronger than before, enabling you to handle such situations better.

Breath

While muscles can be trained and strengthened through physical activity, strengthening vital organs like the heart, lungs, digestive system, liver and kidneys requires a different approach. Your breath is the only pathway here; there's no alternative route to reach them.

As you know, any activity of your body or mind becomes immediately observable in your breath. For instance, your breath quickens when you exert yourself or feel anxious or are angry.

Conversely, you can induce changes in your body and mind by controlling your breath.

It's important to recognise that your breath isn't merely an exchange of oxygen and carbon dioxide but a powerful tool for achieving health and happiness when breathed well. I'm not suggesting you don't know how to breathe, but rather how to breathe well.

If you're feeling anxious or angry, you can quickly feel calmer by intentionally taking long, deep breaths. Simply inhale for a count of eight, hold your breath for four counts, exhale for ten counts and then wait for four counts before inhaling again. Count slowly in your mind and ensure smooth, comfortable breathing. Notice the change after repeating this six to eight times and you may continue until you feel better.

Pranayama is a yogic practice of using your breath to influence your body and mind. In Sanskrit, *'Prana'* means breath and *'yama'* means control. *Pranayama* involves techniques for breathing that incorporate body postures known as *Asanas* and finger positions known as *Mudras*.

Specific combinations of *Asanas*, *Mudras*, and breathing techniques can energise your vital organs, spinal cord, brain and nervous system.

Conversely, awkward body postures, coupled with the finger positions used for swiping and texting, along with emotionally-charged breathing patterns while using your phone or watching TV, can have the opposite effect, potentially harming your health.

Pranayama can aid in detoxifying your body, provided you limit your intake of toxins through food and nerve stimulants like tobacco, alcohol, and even coffee.

Even if you're not feeling well enough for regular physical exercise, you can still practice *Pranayama* to expedite your recovery.

Pranayama can significantly enhance your energy levels throughout the day. However, it's essential for your physical body to support this increased energy output, or you may encounter problems. It's akin to fitting a high-power engine into a smaller car, which may lead to collapse after running fast for a couple of miles. Therefore, physical fitness is crucial; without it, there is little point in enhancing your energy levels beyond a certain point.

Since proper guidance is essential to perform *Pranayama* correctly, I won't delve into the details here. I recommend consulting a Yoga instructor for this. *Pranayama* may be practised anywhere, anytime, and it's easy to learn with the right guidance.

Yoga practices are comprehensive and inclusive. Originating in ancient India, Yoga means 'union.'

Through practices such as *Asanas* (body postures) to improve strength, flexibility, and balance, *Pranayama* to enhance energy levels and the mind, and Meditation to train and elevate the mind and YOU, you can achieve harmony with everything around you, experiencing ease, grace, and happiness.

Food

Food is an integral part of your life, from the day you are born until your last breath, and every day in between.

Good food is essential to maintain ease and ensure smooth, long-lasting functioning of your body, just like the right fuel for your car. Would you ever consider filling your car with low-quality fuel?

What you eat, when you eat, and how you eat are all crucial factors in shaping your physical health.

As you know, the food industry is highly commercialised, often prioritising financial gains over health benefits. The precise combination of salt, sugar, and fat, along with sensations like crunchiness and creaminess, encourages frequent consumption and larger quantities. Food advertisements and packaging amplify these effects, making even junk food tempting.

It's important to consider food as the most important element for nourishing your body, not a source of entertainment.

Every creature on the planet, even tiny ants, knows instinctively what to eat for nourishment. They don't rely on food advertisements, consult with nutritionists, or read the fine print on food packaging.

How do you determine the best food for you?

Listen to your body and observe how you feel after eating. The food that leaves you feeling agile, energetic, and at ease is the best choice for you, not necessarily what your mind desires.

In many parts of the world, people consume food that has been cooked several days or weeks earlier, preserved with chemicals, and kept in cold storage. Eating such food is one of the easiest ways to compromise your health and well-being.

The most common excuses for not having a healthy diet are 'I don't have time' or 'I can't cook well.' However, understanding the importance of your body to achieve your life goals should motivate you to overcome these excuses.

Learning to cook healthy and tasty food is similar to learning any other skill in life, such as language, science, music, cycling, swimming, or driving. Once you start cooking well—it will bring you joy, much like any other hobby.

Preparing good food with interest and involvement and sharing it with your family or friends, can enhance both your health and relationships. However, if you cook reluctantly for yourself or others, such food may not promote health and well-being for anyone.

Shall we delve into more nuances of food?

Would you ever accept an offer in which someone gives you anything you desire in exchange for your life?

Most likely not, right?

It is because your life is incredibly precious to you. If you're uncertain, try holding your breath for as long as you can and notice how you feel as time passes. If you haven't already, please give it a try.

You'd be willing to exchange anything you possess for a breath of air, wouldn't you?

It's not just you; even a tiny ant values its life immensely. If you're not convinced, observe its struggle and effort to escape when you gently press it with one of your fingers.

Consider a slice of tomato or cucumber you eat. In order to thrive and reproduce, it employs its texture and seeds, not with the intention of becoming your meal. They relinquish their purpose and life for your nourishment. Would you be willing to make such a sacrifice for anyone, even those you love dearly?

I agree—except for plants, every life form on this planet must consume another life or its valuable produce to survive. Take only what you need for nutrition—nothing more. It doesn't befit a civilised, evolved human to indulge—whether in food or anything else—at the cost of other lives.

What to eat :

- Incorporate 30-40 percent vegetables into your diet, including fruits, leafy greens, sprouts, and cooked or raw vegetables, as they provide essential vitamins and minerals. Always consume raw food before eating cooked food.

- Another 30 percent should consist of protein-rich foods such as curd, cheese, and pulses, which support muscle growth and repair.

- The remaining portion should come from carbohydrates such as rice, bread, and potatoes, which provide energy for daily activities.

- Sweets, and deep-fried foods offer no real nutritional value. You may have them occasionally, but only for pleasure.

- Avoid processed or frozen foods, alcohol, tobacco, or anything that stimulates the nervous system. These items contain more toxins, requiring your body to work harder and longer to process or eliminate them, which strains your vital organs and drains your energy.

- While nerve stimulants may offer temporary relief from reality, once their effects wear off, you'll likely feel worse than before. They can lead to dependence and addiction, even something as seemingly harmless as a cup of coffee.

When to eat :

- Ensure you eat at regular intervals. When you're indoors—at home or work—you might not feel hungry. However, waiting until you're genuinely hungry can lead to overeating.

- Have a nutritious breakfast to fuel your day and an early dinner around sunset for restful sleep and a refreshed start the next day.

- Aim for a four to five-hour gap between meals. Avoid filling your stomach completely and stop eating when you still feel like having a bit more. This practice enhances digestion and helps maintain energy levels.

- Eat only when you're not feeling angry or depressed, but rather energised, physically and mentally light. If not, it's better to skip the meal. If you must eat, opt for fruits or vegetables.

- Avoid drinking water with your meals to prevent dilution of digestive enzymes. Instead, drink water forty minutes before or after eating.

- Aim to consume 40 ml (in low-humidity areas) to 50 ml (in high-humidity areas) of fluids per kilogram of body weight every day. Opt for warm water whenever possible.

How to eat:

- Before starting your meal, take a moment to pause. Acknowledge that everything on your plate has its own life and purpose. Many lives, both human and non-human, have contributed their efforts to bring it to your plate in its current form. Reflect on this journey and express gratitude to all involved.

- Sit quietly, setting aside distractions and even your thoughts, savour each flavor, chew every bite at least twenty times to aid digestion, and avoid wasting even a bit.

All of these practices will help you consume only what you need for nutrition, reduce the quantity you eat, and enhance the benefits for your health and well-being.

Water and air quality are crucial for your well-being. Strive to find sources of good-quality water and ensure access to clean air wherever possible.

Vegetarian vs Non-Vegetarian

Even ants seem to instinctively know what food is best for them—yet we humans are still full of questions. Which diet offers more vitamins? What about protein content? Which one promotes strength and stamina? Which is better for the heart, brain, or reproductive system? And beyond personal health, which diet is more environmentally friendly?

There are a lot of questions. Let's explore the facts, which can provide guidance rather than a prescription.

Let's start with anatomy. Carnivores are built to swallow chunks of flesh, relying on strong stomach acids to digest meat and neutralise harmful bacteria. They also possess short intestinal tracts and colons, enabling the swift passage of meat through their bodies before it spoils and poses health risks.

On the other hand, herbivores—including humans and other mammals—begin digestion primarily in the mouth. Unlike carnivores, they don't depend on strong stomach acids to break down pre-chewed fruits and vegetables. As a result, human stomach acid is comparatively weaker.

Humans have significantly longer intestinal tracts than carnivores. While this allows for better digestion of fibre and nutrient absorption from plant-based foods, it also poses risks when consuming meat. The extended journey through the digestive system provides bacteria in meat with ample time to multiply, increasing the risk of food poisoning and colon cancer.

Contrary to popular belief, the average plant-eater gets sufficient protein—and it's often healthier than animal protein. Compared to typical non-vegetarian diets, vegetarian diets are very comprehensive in meeting your vitamin requirements because they include a variety of fruits, vegetables, and grains. However, vitamin D—crucial for overall health—is not naturally abundant in food. The best way to maintain healthy levels is by spending 15 to 20 minutes in sunlight each day.

Many world-class athletes on vegetarian diets are living proof that strength and endurance don't depend on meat. The world's strongest man—who lifted over 500 kilograms and walked—follows a vegetarian diet, as do several Olympic medalists. Even many ultra-marathon runners who cover distances more than 100 kilometres, thrive on plant-based nutrition. A vegetarian diet won't let you down here.

When it comes to reproductive abilities, focused research on men has shown that plant-based foods enhance the quality and quantity of erections. I believe both men and women will equally enjoy this.

Meat consumption is linked to a 50 percent higher risk of heart disease and a threefold increase in the risk of colon cancer compared to plant-based diets. It also carries toxins released by animals under extreme fear and pain during slaughter. If you have ever heard the scream or witnessed the struggle of an animal being killed, you may never eat its flesh again.

Moreover, the hormones administered to farm animals for rapid growth and enhanced meat flavour can lead to hormone imbalances and related health issues, particularly in growing children.

Mother Earth is facing a severe resource shortage due to the significant size of the human population and their lifestyle. Over 75 percent of farmland is used for producing meat, dairy, eggs, and fish, even though these foods provide only 20 percent of the world's calories. It is the primary cause of biodiversity destruction and deforestation, while also contributing to 15 percent of all emissions caused by humans, equivalent to emissions from vehicles, ships, and planes combined.

Moreover, animals consume more than 25 percent of the world's freshwater supply, worsening the global water crisis, an increasingly serious threat.

I hope you got the direction if your top priorities are your health and well-being, as well as a sustainable environment for you, other people, and future generations.

Fasting

We've been discussing what food is best for you. Let's take a moment to explore the concept of not eating!

Fasting, when combined with a wholesome diet and an active lifestyle, could further improve your health.

According to Ayurveda, *Ajeernam Bhojanam Visham*, in Sanskrit, means 'eating again without digesting the previous meal is like taking poison.' This emphasises how the same food you enjoyed and expected to nourish you can become harmful when not properly digested.

Fasting involves abstaining from some or all food for a specific period. Typically, people fast for 16 hours daily, undertake a 24-hour fast every two weeks, or opt for longer fasts lasting 48 or even up to 72 hours on special occasions.

Every two weeks, the Yogic system observes *Ekadashi* day, the 11th day of the waxing and waning phases of the moon, which calls for a partial or full fast to purify and rejuvenate the body. As you are aware, fasting is a significant aspect of most religious beliefs.

If you've been eating more than usual during festivals or special occasions, you may start feeling uneasy and lethargic. A 24-hour fast can quickly restore your energy and overall well-being.

Since food provides 20–30 percent of the fluids the body requires, it is quite possible to become dehydrated while fasting. Therefore, it's crucial to consume enough water while fasting.

It's advisable to avoid intense exercise during fasting periods, but low-intensity exercises such as walking, mild yoga, gentle stretching, and housework can enhance the benefits of fasting.

When breaking your fast, it's best not to consume a particularly large meal. Instead, start your normal eating routine again with some fruits, dates, and small snacks.

Fasting can enhance the taste of your food. No doubt, hunger is the best sauce. Moreover, regular fasting reduces temptation over time, making it easier to resist food cravings.

Fasting improves your ability to absorb nutrients and increases growth hormone secretion, which is crucial for growth, recovery, metabolism, muscle strength, and weight loss.

Fasting has been associated with a variety of potential health advantages, including improved blood sugar regulation, reduced inflammation, improved heart health by lowering blood pressure, triglycerides, and cholesterol levels, enhanced brain function, and the prevention of neurodegenerative diseases, tumour growth, and cancer.

I trust you now have sufficient reasons to embrace fasting and enjoy its benefits.

Fasting is not advised for individuals with heart disease, type 2 diabetes, difficulties managing blood sugar, low blood pressure, those attempting to conceive, pregnant or breastfeeding women, individuals who are underweight, older adults, children, or teenagers.

Healthy eating habits and a fit lifestyle are essential prerequisites for fasting. Otherwise, vitamin supplements may be necessary to prevent deficiencies. If you intend to fast for longer than 24 hours or have any underlying medical conditions, it's important to consult your doctor beforehand.

Sleep

Sleep plays a significant role in your physical and mental well-being.

Why is sleep essential?

Your body and mind both require rest to recover, repair, and recharge, enabling them to function efficiently and effectively without experiencing breakdowns. Therefore, reclining to fully rest your body and free up your mind from thoughts can be as beneficial as—or even superior to—sleeping.

However, for most people, it is challenging to set aside their thoughts, making sleep the easiest option. With practice in reducing your thoughts and freeing your mind—as we discussed during meditation—you can certainly improve your ability to achieve restful relaxation without sleep.

You can go without food for a few days, but if you don't sleep for two days, your body and mind will become dysfunctional. If you follow the principles of what, when and how you eat, as we discussed, seven to eight hours of uninterrupted sleep is recommended for your overall well-being. Additionally, as you are aware, meditation can further enhance these benefits.

Many people sleep a lot because they don't have many important things to do in their lives. Remember, too much rest can lead to rust, both physically and mentally. Mental faculties are capable of a continuous, sustained effort; they don't tire like an arm or a leg. All they need is change, not rest, except during sleep.

Your physical and mental health can greatly benefit from adopting a sleep schedule that involves going to bed before 10 o'clock at night and rising around 4 o'clock in the morning. Make the best use of the *Brahma Muhurta*, which begins 1 hour and 36 minutes before sunrise and ends 48 minutes before sunrise at your location.

Avoid using electronic devices for at least the last half-hour before bedtime and the first half-hour after waking up. This practice allows your mind to gradually wind down before sleep and gently wake up, enhancing its overall functioning. Additionally, don't keep your phone or other electronic devices switched on in your bedroom.

If you consume more food than necessary, especially if it contains toxins, consume alcohol, tobacco or use other nerve stimulants, you will certainly need additional sleep to recover, repair, and recharge.

Moreover, if you also sleep less, you are damaging your health and heading towards disaster. I hope you are not doing this and will never do it.

Self-Care

Your body, like any other machine, requires protection from the external environment to prevent damage and ensure proper functioning. The more sophisticated and capable the machine, the more attention and care it needs to maintain its effectiveness and efficiency.

Personal hygiene should be a top priority. To cleanse your physical body and balance your energy body, it's recommended to bathe at least once per day with flowing water from head to toe. Bathing in running water is ideal. If it is stagnant water, you may squat, dip yourself completely, and rise multiple times to create a similar effect. If you're using your bathroom, consider using a bucket filled with water and pouring it over yourself with a mug. The larger the mug, the better it is. Newly washed clothes are better to wear for any day.

A clean and organised environment, both at work and at home, is essential for your productivity and overall well-being. A tidy home, a well-kept kitchen, a serene bedroom, an orderly desk, and functional tools—cleanliness and order in everything you touch, hear, see, and smell—can boost your energy levels and foster positivity, often referred to as positive energy.

Conversely, clutter, dirt, unpleasant odours, and noise can drain you and those around you, creating what we call negative energy. Keeping a neat and clean environment requires dedication and effort, but the rewards are substantial.

Dressing suitably is crucial to protecting your body from heat, cold, moisture, dust, and dirt. Your clothing should be comfortable, allowing you to move freely without feeling self-conscious or restricted, ensuring you can function effectively. Cotton fabric is ideal for most situations, except for sports where specialised materials may be more appropriate.

No matter where you are, people will appreciate you based on the energy and positivity you exude—not by the colour of your skin or the shape of your face.

One of the simplest ways to enhance this energy, step into your role, boost your confidence, and lift your spirits is through your clothing. Whether you're at work, social events, religious gatherings, or even at home, your clothing makes a statement before your intelligence, character, or behaviour.

Making a strong first impression sets the foundation for subsequent interactions, such as the initial meeting, presentation, key discussions, proposals, negotiations, or performances. Remember, you never get a second chance to make a first impression.

Dressing well presents you as a significant, effective, and reliable individual. Conversely, if you don't, people might see you as careless, ineffective, or unimportant. Maintain a classy appearance wherever you go by investing in a few quality items rather than opting for many lower-quality ones.

I recall a research study conducted by a major coffee brand to understand their customers' preferences among the different coffee varieties they offered.

At that time, they had three types available: Classic, Gold, and Premium. Classic was the most affordable, Gold was priced in the middle, and Premium was the most expensive option.

Classic coffee came in a standard printed plastic wrapper with red and yellow colours, while Gold, despite being in plastic packaging, had a rich light green and gold dual-tone design. Premium was packaged in a carton with a combination of black and silver colours and glossy lamination.

They filled all three types of packets with the same coffee powder as part of the experiment and gave them to a sample group of customers. After two weeks, they collected their feedback, and it was revealing.

Most customers found the classic taste to be ordinary, while they thought the gold was better. However, they believed the premium coffee to have a distinctly rich aroma and flavour, despite all of them containing the same coffee powder.

This is how packaging and appearance have an impact. It applies to the way you dress and carry yourself.

Avoid revealing your body in ways that attract undue attention or indulgence from others. Others need not concern themselves with your body, which is your personal and exclusive asset, but rather with your skills and abilities.

You may argue that it's entirely your choice. Is that really the case?

In the case of women, it's often evident that the way they are expected to dress and appear and present themselves is largely shaped by male preferences. These preferences are then marketed and promoted as fashion and beauty trends to cater to such tastes. Despite the challenges associated with such dress codes, societal pressure begins from a young age, compelling women to conform to them.

Is it truly a matter of choice or freedom, or rather a subtle compulsion to conform to social norms?

The same holds true for men, especially when it comes to the expectations of 'power dressing' in professional or social settings—often at the cost of comfort, regardless of weather conditions or other inconveniences.

For adequate protection and privacy, it's advisable to dress in a way that covers your body from your shoulders to well below your knees. Additionally, wearing a spot of colour on your forehead can help others engage with you, at the highest point in your body—your forehead.

Even if the other person hasn't covered their body adequately or doesn't have a spot on their forehead, it's important to maintain similar interactions with them. Engaging with another person may lead to indulgence and affect the sincerity and intent of the interaction as it delves deeper into their physical presence. This affects your energy body and weakens your other senses, similarly impacting the other person.

Your life energy has the power to affect another person at any time or place, and vice versa. Additionally, various energies in the environment can also influence you. During activities such as eating or physical intimacy, you are more receptive to these energies because you are naturally more open at such times. Therefore, it's advisable to engage in these activities only in appropriate settings.

In general, it's advisable to avoid physical contact with others, including when greeting them. Physical contact may result in an exchange of energy, which may result in both physical and psychological effects.

This is why the Indian cultural practice of *Namaste*, where individuals greet one other with folded hands, is preferred. *Namaste*, derived from Sanskrit, means 'I bow to the life within you,' signifying respect and acknowledgement of the life force within each individual.

If you experience discomfort after spending time in a particular place or coming into proximity with someone, consider cleansing your energy. Bathing in running water from head to toe can help, as can exposure to natural wind.

You can also use fire, such as an oil lamp or lit camphor, passing it along your body from head to toe, keeping it at a safe distance from your skin, a couple of times, to restore energy balance faster. It's important to note that you would need someone's assistance to perform this cleansing using fire on yourself.

Why do we visit places of worship?

To align and enhance our life energy for efficiency, peace of mind, and happiness. These places are specially designed and maintained for this purpose, following a code of conduct for everyone. When everyone comes to such a place with a similar mindset and purpose, it works even better.

The visuals, vocal and instrumental sounds, flowers, lamps, fire, aromas, holy water, and specially prepared food—are all part of the design and processes implemented there. The prayers associated with the beliefs also work because your mind is your greatest source of power.

Consuming food with minimal toxins, maintaining body hygiene, dressing appropriately, adopting proper posture, and maintaining a less occupied mind are all essential when interacting with such energy centres to maximise their benefits. This is why people often make dietary and lifestyle changes before visiting these places. Following the guidelines and behaving appropriately in these spaces is crucial—not just for your own well-being but also for the collective harmony of all who visit.

A Healthy Body

We've addressed every aspect of maintaining a relaxed, effective, and well-functioning body to ensure it never prevents you from fulfilling your needs and desires.

How do you know it's working for you?

From the moment you wake up until you go to bed, you'll feel consistently energetic. Once you settle into bed, you'll quickly drift into a restful sleep and wake up early with the energy and enthusiasm necessary to seize the day. You'll find yourself completing tasks that would normally take weeks in just a matter of days. Once you've experienced it, you'll never settle for anything less.

These days, there are instruments available to measure your body's age. If you're physically fit, your body age will closely reflect your actual age, which is a good sign. However, if you're not in good physical health, your body age may be much older than your actual age, indicating premature aging. Is that something anyone would like?

On the other hand, if you're very fit, your body age will be significantly younger than your actual age, giving you more time and energy to pursue your life goals. Moreover, compared to peers of the same age, you'll appear noticeably younger. This is the ideal outcome to strive for. While being fit and looking good may come naturally at a young age, maintaining it as you grow older demands increased effort and attention.

To access and experience anything, your body is your only instrument. The specific chemicals generated within your body determine whether you feel happy or sad. Physical exercise, nutritious food, gentle sunlight, restful sleep, self-care, listening to music, being with nature, mindfulness, meditation, achieving tasks and goals, helping others, socialising, laughter, and expressing affection through kissing or cuddling—all of these actions trigger the release of happiness chemicals in your body. They collectively contribute to your overall health, happiness, and lasting vitality.

Keeping yourself fit allows you to excel at work, manage household chores, enjoy your favorite sports, travel wherever you wish, play with your children or grandchildren, and walk without support as you age. It enables you to independently pursue what matters most to you without relying on others.

Good health grants you a remarkable degree of freedom. You won't realise its value until you no longer have it. By maintaining your health, you not only benefit yourself but also support your loved ones in achieving their goals, rather than depending on their assistance. Your health is indeed one of the greatest gifts you can offer them.

Even if you possess everything else, you'll eventually realise you have nothing without your health. I hope you remember the Himalayan trekking experience we discussed. The version of you who sacrificed health to accumulate wealth might willingly forfeit all riches to regain health, but it's often too late. Health comes first—your true companion until your last breath.

You must take excellent care of your health so that you rarely need to worry about it.

Make this a lifelong commitment.

Step 4

Love and Relationships

Genuine connections flourish when they're built on mutual support, respect, trust, and sharing. It's essential to make a consistent effort to build, strengthen, and maintain relationships.

In the last three steps, we covered the key elements of your happiness and explored both theory and practice behind them. It was all about you—focusing on ensuring that you don't hinder your own success.

Naturally, it's important to continually practice them to evolve and adapt to each new role that unfolds in your life. Life does not become easier—you grow stronger.

Do you remember how reluctant you were to brush your teeth when you were a child? You probably needed encouragement or even faced punishment to do it regularly. Can you imagine skipping brushing your teeth even for one day now?

You know how it feels if you forget your toothbrush when you travel. You'll make sure to buy a toothbrush for the next morning before anything else, right? Even when unwell and unable to get up, you somehow manage to brush your teeth because it has become a part of your life through its benefits.

When you regularly engage in physical exercise, *Pranayama*, and meditation, you won't skip them, even for a day because you experience how they enhance both your day and your life. You no longer need rewards or punishments to motivate you anymore. Those days are over.

If you can't influence even one person, including yourself, for your own benefit, you'll miss out on much in life.

If your physical and mental health don't support your efforts to fulfill responsibilities at home or work, you experience stress. When stress continues to mount, it doesn't merely add up, it multiplies, pushing you toward a breaking point.

It spreads throughout your body, disrupting the healthy function of vital organs such as the heart, liver, kidneys, lungs, and stomach. It can manifest as anger, anxiety, jealousy, ego, irritation, and feelings of failure. This is how the most capable life on the planet miserably fails.

One simple way to reduce stress is to complete the easy tasks first, like fixing a home appliance, getting your vehicle or work tools repaired, replying to important messages, sending a courier, paying bills, or calling a friend. Finishing these small tasks reduces your to-do list, frees up mental space, lowers stress, and allows you to focus on bigger, more important things.

In the next four steps, we will explore other critical aspects of your success, including the people and things around you, though you remain the most vital element, and the practices from the last three steps will greatly support you.

Love

As discussed, loving what you do (LoWyD) is crucial for your happiness.

But what exactly is love?

Is it something you intentionally do?

No, it isn't.

It's the feeling you experience when you embrace something outside of yourself and accept it as a part of yourself.

Now, onto the next question: How do you differentiate between what is within you and what lies outside of you?

You might believe that your identity is confined to your skin and all that lies within it, while anything outside of that is considered part of something or someone else. Although this perception helps you to survive, it hinders your ability to grow and explore life beyond these boundaries.

One of the greatest limitations humans encounter is the idea of possession, which categorises things as either 'mine' or 'not mine,' often leading to conflicts.

What about your parents, siblings, spouse, in-laws, friends, teachers, colleagues, and many others who have helped shape who you are today and what you have? And what about the trees providing you with oxygen to breathe, the rivers supplying you with water to drink, the plants giving their lives to become your food, the farmers cultivating them for you, and others working in various capacities to make your day? What about the work you do to meet your needs or fulfill your desires?

Are they part of you or outside you?

You will feel a deep sense of harmony with them and truly experience love for them when you stop viewing something as either yours or someone else's, and instead, see it as a part of yourself. The mother of all feelings!

The Indian philosopher and spiritual scholar Swami Vivekananda once travelled to America. During his visit, an English woman approached him, expressing her desire to marry him. Swami Vivekananda inquired about her reasoning.

She explained that she found Swami's wisdom fascinating and wished to have a child as wise as him through marrying him.

Swami smiled at her and responded with these words: 'Since you are drawn to my wisdom alone, fulfilling your wish is simple. Marriage and the process of bringing a child into the world take time, and there's no guarantee the child will have the intelligence you expect. However, I have a suggestion that can fulfil your wish immediately. Consider accepting me as your son instead. By doing so, you become my mother, and your wish for a wise child like me will also be fulfilled.'

No matter your profession— homemaker, teacher, farmer, doctor, mechanic, lawyer, engineer, or in any other role—you can only provide the best for others if you love them. As a mother to them. You'll never feel burdened by your work or supporting colleagues, family, or friends, or others because you're doing it for someone deeply ingrained within yourself. Instead, you'll find happiness and joy in all these activities.

You won't ever need to say 'I love you' to any of them because it will be apparent from your behaviour and actions. Don't expect anything in return because it is a feel, not a deal.

Are love and affection the same?

Not exactly.

Love entails a profound emotional connection characterised by commitment and care for others' well-being. Affection, however, refers to the fondness and closeness expressed through gestures such as holding hands, hugging, kissing, or offering kind words. Affection doesn't necessarily imply a deep emotional bond or long-term commitment like love does.

To love and be loved is what all people long for most.

Relationships

Maintaining positive relationships with your partner, spouse, children, extended family, friends, neighbors, work associates, and society greatly contributes to your happiness. Remember, relationships hold more significance than material comforts in the happiness formula we discussed before. Happy individuals prioritise and nurture their relationships, which, in turn, enhances their happiness further.

Many individuals form relationships with others, hoping to gain something in return. Even with God. However, this approach doesn't foster healthy relationships. Genuine connections flourish when they're built on mutual support and sharing. In such cases, support is offered even without explicitly being asked.

Don't feel disheartened if people only reach out to you when they need assistance. If they had another choice, they might not have approached you. Do your best to offer assistance when asked, but it's even better to offer help before it's requested. Treat it as a chance to elevate yourself.

It is not ingratitude if they don't stay in touch with you; they may simply not want to burden you if no further support is needed. When someone supports you even when they're facing their own struggles, it's not just help—it's an expression of love.

Mutual respect and trust are the cornerstones of strong relationships.

Are they different or do they rely on each other?

Respect involves recognising and valuing the qualities, abilities, and achievements of others. It involves treating them with dignity, fairness, honesty, kindness, and compassion, regardless of differences, and valuing their opinions, boundaries, and autonomy. Respect forms the foundation for trust.

Trust, on the other hand, involves openness, transparency, and reliability cultivated through consistent behaviour, communication, and mutual respect. It enhances both the efficiency and effectiveness of everything we do together.

These qualities help you to set clear expectations, keep your promises, and sincerely apologise when you make mistakes. Sometimes, you apologise not because you're wrong, but because you value the relationship more than being right. In either case, genuinely ask them what you can do to make things right. Remember, relationships are fragile, so handle them with care!

Consider the common scenario of people arriving late to meetings, social events, or personal appointments. Their delay often inconveniences everyone else, causing frustration, discomfort, and wasting time for all involved. Despite sincere apologies and familiar excuses like bad weather, traffic, or getting lost, the underlying issue is often a prioritisation of their own convenience. Even such common behaviour undermines the foundation of trust and mutual respect. Their long story or big sorry can't undo the impact.

Sharing resources—like your home, vehicle, food, or thoughtful gifts—encourages cooperation and strengthens relationships. It's equally important to ensure fair exchange for what you receive, so you're not consistently taking more than you give.

Think of it as a bank account: you must deposit before you withdraw, or you'll end up with a negative balance, which can strain even close relationships. It's always better to have others owe you rather than being indebted to them. Giving is also a skill that must be consciously developed and practised.

If you're invited to lunch or dinner—even by a close friend or relative—consider bringing a gift for the host. It could be something homemade or something you pick up on your way. This simple gesture not only allows you to contribute, and it also enhances the joy of the occasion.

Whenever possible, consider potlucks to encourage participation, sharing, and the spirit of giving. After all, strong relationships are built on give and take—the true magic lies in giving a little more than you receive.

When Hurricane Katrina struck the southern coast of the United States of America, I happened to be in Dallas.

That week, while flying out of the city, the seat next to mine was occupied by a young man from one of the worst-affected areas. He was wearing a wristband issued by the authorities to receive better assistance with travel and food, as he had lost everything.

During the flight, he showed the wristband to the air hostess in the hope of receiving a meal, but she had to apologise as the flight didn't serve food.

I had packed a burger at the airport for lunch, so I offered it to him. He looked relieved but surprised me by cutting the burger in half and returning one portion along with a small tetra pack of apple juice he had obtained from somewhere.

He smiled at me and said, 'Let us share.'

The quality of your relationships significantly impacts the quality of your life experiences. It's not merely about making friends or being close to family members, but about building and nurturing relationships with people you genuinely like and who add value to your life. Finding such individuals is hard, and retaining them is even harder. If you don't value them, they will simply move on without you even noticing. It's essential to consistently work to build, strengthen, and maintain meaningful relationships.

Conversely, surrounding yourself with lazy and unhappy people can influence you to adopt similar attitudes. Surrounding yourself with positive and action-oriented individuals is a better choice. If a relationship leaves you feeling inadequate or envious, it may be time to gradually distance yourself from it. If you don't belong in a place, you may not know how to speak or behave there. You should leave social gatherings feeling energised and inspired, not exhausted and agitated.

New people will always enter your life, and some old ones may leave. Being friendly with the happy, compassionate towards the sad, learning from the wise, and ignoring the wicked can offer helpful guidance for relationships. You are as good as the company you keep.

Many people expect their love and relationships with others to mirror the unconditional love they receive from their dog. However, it's important to understand the difference. A dog will always love you, regardless of the circumstances; it will wag its tail when you give it attention, whine when you don't, and bark if someone tries to claim or threaten you. This unwavering affection, even when the rest of the world may not regard you highly, is a classic example of loyalty that nurtures your mental image.

No one can support you in the same way because neither humans nor other animals are built or naturally inclined to do so. It cannot serve as a benchmark for what you expect from relationships with other people. Such expectations can limit your interactions with humans, making your life revolve mostly around your dog(s) and preventing you from fully living your own life. It won't let your dog live its life either, even though it will keep entertaining you like an ever-affectionate, never-growing child.

You may have some people who nurture your self-image, though nowhere close to the loyalty of your dog, by frequently texting or calling you, wishing you well on every occasion, liking and commenting on your social media posts, and praising you regularly. However, this behaviour is not a standard for good relationships as they often expect the same from you. Such relationships require significant effort and time to maintain, and a single misstep may cause them to fail.

Good relationships don't rely on constant texting, talking, meeting, or gifting to sustain them. There's no need for image-nursing tactics to feel better when you're secure in who you are.

Is social media a force for good?

As you know, nothing is inherently good or bad. If something yields positive outcomes, it's considered good; conversely, if it results in negative consequences, it's deemed bad.

Beyond its original purpose of fostering connection and communication, social media has evolved into a space filled with superficial messages, trivial videos, pointless conversations, targeted advertisements, fake news, scandals, and polarisation. These platforms are meticulously designed to captivate and engage users, often exploiting their interests and vulnerabilities for various purposes. Since users don't pay for these services, they themselves become the product, sold to advertisers.

In such a setting, where everyone is free to hold their own opinions and facts, few laws, rules, or standards of behaviour exist. It violates the laws of the neighbourhood, society, and even the government due to a lack of responsibility or shared understanding of reality. Thoughts and emotions are communicated rapidly in such an environment and fake news spreads much faster than the truth.

Constantly checking messages, scanning for likes, and responding to comments can lead to addiction, stealing your ability to concentrate and focus both at work and at home. These distractions significantly impair creativity, efficiency, and productivity. Moreover, excessive social media use has made users anxious, fearful, fragile, depressed, less self-assured, risk-averse, and even less romantic. Consequently, rates of self-harm and suicide have also increased.

Social media platforms serve as powerful networking and communication tools in the digital era. Make the best use of them to your advantage, but remain mindful not to let them enslave you, control you, damage your relationships, or undermine your happiness and well-being.

Marriage

The association between a husband and wife is one of the most unique, significant, and profound human relationships for most people. A good marriage is one of the life factors most strongly and consistently linked with happiness. Conversely, the opposite holds true as well.

Why do people choose to marry?

Many people get married because it's a social norm and others are doing it as well. Studies reveal that the fundamental human need for reliable companionship often remains unmet, whether married or not.

If you find yourself bored with your own company, imagine how dull it might be for someone else. When two bored individuals come together, it can become incredibly monotonous, don't you think?

Yes, hormones might drive you to seek companionship with the opposite sex. However, if this is the main driving force, there are likely better alternatives than marriage. Considering the overpopulation of the planet and the strain on natural resources, choosing not to reproduce can also be a valid option.

Please don't misunderstand me. I'm not suggesting that there aren't any valid reasons to get married, but the obvious ones may not always be the right ones.

I hope you recall our discussion on the prominence of masculine traits—analytical, logical, decisive, assertive, independent, individualistic, self-assured in men and feminine traits—intuition, creativity, receptiveness, nurturing, grace, sensitivity, compassion in women.

These qualities complement one other, with men excelling in some areas and women excelling in others. This is the law of nature, where everything works in harmony rather than against each other. Contradictions exist only in our minds, particularly in untrained minds.

When you form a union with someone of the opposite sex, it's an opportunity to share yourself more deeply and meaningfully, achieving beyond what you can do alone. By combining both masculine and feminine traits, you draw upon each other's resources and potential, surpassing limitations and maximising life's opportunities. This is the primary reason for getting married.

However, marriage also exposes weaknesses and wounds, inviting pain and shame, but providing both partners with more opportunities for learning, growth, and healing.

If, for any reason, this doesn't appeal to you, it's absolutely fine to remain single.

It's a natural progression to move from depending on your parents during childhood to gaining independence in your teenage years, and eventually embracing interdependence with everything and everyone around you to achieve beyond your individual capabilities. Life, by its very nature, is interdependent, with families, communities, and institutions all built on mutual reliance. That's why marriage is considered a privilege and highly respected in the social context.

However, many marriages restrict the freedom of both partners to pursue what truly matters to them. Such a marriage loses all its meaning. Like in all aspects of life, including this one, success hinges on your character, commitment, and competence—what I like to call the 3 Cs.

Choosing a Partner

'Made for each other,' 'my soul mate,' 'the perfect partner'—you've probably heard these phrases many times, though they exist more in your imagination than in reality. Remember, you're only perfect on the day you're born and the day you die. Life in between is what we're discussing.

Don't search for the perfect partner because such people don't exist on the planet. No one will ever fully meet your expectations. You could behave like an ideal partner, which is what most people do. It's not that hard to pretend about your character and commitment, though not about your competence.

Pretending to be skilled—whether it's sports, singing, playing an instrument, driving, or cooking is nearly impossible because when asked to perform, your incompetence is exposed. As a result, most people won't do it.

You can only evaluate a potential partner's character and commitment, which may not reflect their true selves due to pretence, not their abilities to create a successful relationship.

If it's your first experience of exploring and expanding into someone else, it may make you feel they are the perfect partner for you, like no one else on Earth. This can make moving on and leaving that person extremely difficult, even in the face of many challenges. You might end up sacrificing important aspects of your life to sustain the relationship, which can lead to conflicts later on.

On the other hand, if you can leave the relationship for any reason, it will enhance your ability to view such relationships objectively and make you a more loving and lovable person.

Even if you know each other well before marriage, it might not help much because the pretenses tend to dissolve only after the marriage, revealing who you truly are. This applies to both partners.

Real life begins at that point, and you are left with no choice but to invest the time and effort necessary to make the relationship work. If both partners are not willing to do so, even if you have chosen the smartest person for your life, it may not help, and the relationship can face serious difficulties.

I'm not being negative—just fairly practical.

What you once liked and admired in your partner during your dating days can later become thorns in your married life. For example, Preethi initially loved Anand's passion for playing the guitar, and she even joined him occasionally with his local music band. However, as their life progressed, Preethi became upset when Anand prioritised his musical pursuits over helping their children with their studies.

'You knew me before,' 'We agreed to this,' and 'Do you want me to change now?' may feel like valid thoughts, but they won't help you move forward. You must change if your life demands it.

You may seek a partner who is reliable, independent, loving, attractive, and romantic. Additionally, someone who is family-oriented, manages household tasks, supports your life goals, engages in meaningful conversations about them, encourages your pursuits, and is socially adept.

Yet, finding someone who embodies all these qualities can be a challenge. Hence, you typically prioritise certain qualities and make compromises on others when choosing a partner.

Even with careful consideration and selection, you won't get very far because, as time goes on, both your and your partner's priorities are likely to change.

Over time, attraction and chemistry often yield to emotional stability, maturity, independence, and grace. Shared values and goals—whether related to family, career, health, or personal growth—along with a genuine appreciation for each other's efforts and achievements, may become more important.

Maintaining a strong relationship requires consistently observing, adapting, and realigning their priorities. The relationship can become difficult if the fundamental expectations of men as protectors and providers and women as nurturers are challenged, even though compromises can be made on many other fronts.

In marriage, you'll need the skills to manage the expected duties of being a husband or wife, son-in-law or daughter-in-law, father, or mother, along with many other expanded roles and responsibilities. Additionally, you'll encounter situations such as social obligations, extended family dynamics, child discipline, educational needs, financial responsibilities, and more.

Only when you handle such roles and face real-life situations will you realise your own shortcomings. It's impossible to prepare and be fully ready in advance. Given the differing life experiences between you and your partner, you'll likely have varying preferences regarding all these aspects, which can easily lead to conflicts.

There is no such thing as a perfect relationship, so avoid comparing yours to others'. No one's life is flawless, with everything consistently going right. Can you name three happily married couples who could offer you guidance?

It's a difficult task, isn't it?

Unlike in other areas of life, you may not find even a single perfect example.

It's not about simply agreeing, compromising, or adjusting for harmony, as that alone cannot foster good relationships. Instead, you must be willing to disagree, point out flaws, and support each other's growth and change—all with love and respect. Love is genuine and enduring when it's given with awareness of the other person's flaws.

After all, love and affection matter far more than perfection.

Commitment

The passionate love you feel for each other typically fades within three months to two years of marriage. As this phase passes, you might begin to feel that your spouse is no longer in love with you. However, it's the compassionate love between two firmly committed individuals that nurtures strong relationships and enduring marriages.

While compassionate love may seem less intense than passionate love, it has the strength to endure a lifetime. It's what shines in the lives of those who make a deliberate effort to love each other, their families, and their children, despite obstacles and the inevitable changes that come with age and circumstances.

Marriage is a long-term commitment—often spanning twenty-five to thirty years, especially if you choose to have children. It's not a sprint but a marathon. A couple remaining together, particularly as good parents, is crucial for the overall development and well-being of their children.

Children observe closely. They follow your example more than your advice. Therefore, it's essential to set a positive example for them in terms of support, self-control, dedication, perseverance, honesty, respect, love, and compassion. The success of your children depends more on these qualities than on the financial support, comforts, or conveniences you provide for them.

You'll often find people from humble beginnings becoming highly successful and inspiring, while those raised in privileged environments—with every resource for success—can still end up unfulfilled and unhappy.

Children cannot develop physically, intellectually, or emotionally without proper parental support. A significant percentage of children live in families with confused relationships, domestic violence, single parents or step-parents. The denials, deprivations, cruelties, and injustices these children face will have significant adverse impacts on their development and their ability to lead fulfilling, socially responsible lives as adults.

The scars of these early experiences often persist into adulthood. Many troubled and violent adult lives can be traced back to the childhood abuse they suffered. And that—knowingly or unknowingly—could become the greatest injustice you inflict not just on your children, but on the world itself.

The majority of programming over the past few decades has focused on teaching us how to break up rather than how to make marriages work. This has led to pitting men and women against each other, downplaying the importance of parents staying together to raise their children, devaluing sacrifice and commitment, glorification of the single and carefree lifestyle, and placing undue emphasis on sex. Beware—'toxic singles' are major influencers here.

Far less attention has been given to the fundamentals that truly sustain relationships—like effective communication, conflict resolution, and understanding the impacts of separation on oneself, loved ones, and especially children and recognising the importance of hard work in marriage—rather than solely focusing on partner selection, romance, or sex—contributing to catalysing divorces.

Before laying eggs, birds diligently search for a safe and suitable nesting spot. They may choose an abandoned nest, reinforce its structure, or build a new one if needed. To ensure the safety and well-being of their young, both the male and female work together with remarkable coordination. The female carefully incubates the eggs, keeping them warm beneath her wings until they hatch, while the male guards the nest and brings food to support her during this crucial period.

When the eggs hatch, both parents share the responsibility for raising their chicks. They feed them and protect them from predators such as cats and snakes. They shelter the chicks under their wings, shielding them from the cold, wind, and rain. As the chicks grow wings, the parents patiently teach them how to fly and train them to find food, closely guiding them every step of the way.

Although the parents could easily continue feeding their chicks with just a little extra effort, they instead focus on preparing them to survive independently. Eventually, the young birds fly away. The parents neither expect anything in return nor rely on their offspring for care in old age. This trait is shared by other animals as well, as it is a fundamental aspect of the natural order.

However, human beings often struggle with many of these responsibilities, even though, as the most capable life form on the planet, we are expected to fulfil them far better than other species.

Extramarital Relationships

Marriage, as a social institution that binds a couple together for an extended period, contradicts the law of nature. Nature dictates the pursuit of multiple mates and reproduction, as seen in most other life forms on the planet. Any living entity that defies the laws of nature experiences stress, and men and women are no exception.

Although you may feel attracted to other individuals, you often refrain from emotional or physical intimacy due to concerns about potential consequences, yet they remain active in your mind. As you are well aware, it is what runs through your mind that determines both the good and the bad, rather than the actions of the other person. While a physical action like hugging your wife or daughter may seem similar, it's the thoughts in your mind that truly differentiate the experience, right?

Remember, forming emotional connections, fantasising about intimate acts with others, or engaging in sexual conversations can be equally impactful as physically engaging in them.

However, you may find greater happiness if you can pursue your instincts while maintaining healthy relationships with your partners and fulfilling your responsibilities to your children. In fact, embracing such freedom while appreciating human nature can make life simpler and more enjoyable. After all, possessiveness, jealousy, and anger aren't love, are they?

Achieving this balance requires clarity in your thoughts and actions, as well as emotional maturity. Maturity involves exercising self-control to distance yourself from individuals and situations that undermine your values, self-worth, and peace of mind. While this may sound simple, it's often difficult, as many people lack these abilities. Despite your best efforts, you may face challenges that disrupt your happiness.

Additionally, managing multiple relationships and many children requires sharing your resources, which can strain the marriage as an economic institution. As a result, such arrangements are discouraged as inappropriate for humans, through strict social and moral behaviour. It is deeply ingrained in the fabric of every civilised society as a code of conduct, with legal norms established to support and uphold it. Consequently, infidelity frequently emerges as a primary cause of chronic marital conflict.

Extramarital affairs often stem from the desire for attention, to feel special, loved, and important, rather than solely from physical pleasure. These affairs can seem exciting and enjoyable until they are discovered by your partner.

In today's digitally interconnected world, it's relatively easy to uncover such secrets through widely used communication platforms and easily accessible services. Once exposed, the repercussions can be profound and may even permanently shatter your happiness. Your ability to remain composed and resilient may be the only thing that can salvage the relationship.

When an affair is exposed, it's important to engage in constructive conversations that explore the underlying issues. This is the best thing you can do for someone you love, isn't it? Otherwise, does it even matter?

Focus on questions such as what the affair means to your partner, what needs it fulfils that your relationship doesn't, and how it impacts both of you and your children. Avoid making excuses, blaming others, justifying, or minimising it. Avoid questions that provoke anger, embarrassment, or pain, such as whether it was only texting or physical, how often you met, or if the other person was 'better'. This can help bring honesty and openness to your relationship, which may have been lost along the way, long before the affair began.

Healing and forgiveness often begin when the person who had the affair acknowledges their wrongdoing and takes corrective action. However, it's important to respect the partner's need for space and time to process it and not to pressure them for forgiveness or reconciliation. Remember that rebuilding trust takes time, effort, and patience from both partners. It's essential to prioritise open communication, empathy, and mutual respect as you navigate this difficult period in your relationship.

This can even lead to both partners becoming more mentally and physically engaged than before and to a more fulfilling relationship. Every affair has the potential to redefine a relationship. It can either become better than before or turn into a disaster.

It is a risky affair!

The guilt and pain usually arise from hurting the partner but not the act itself because it is a natural temptation and one that may persist. Being mentally or physically involved with another person is not the only way you hurt your partner. Dislike, disrespect, denial, indifference, violence, contempt, and neglecting shared responsibilities could be equally, if not more damaging, in such relationships.

In intimate relationships, love and trust compel you to shed pretence and lower your guard, allowing you to be authentic with each other. This depth of connection cannot be achieved with chocolates, flowers, or gifts. You'll recognise the pain hidden behind their smile, and the affection concealed within their anger. Physical closeness becomes natural. Love dissolves distance—both physical and emotional.

It's impossible to truly enjoy someone else's company or have a meaningful physical relationship without it. Your bodily fluids may mix, but not your souls. More than your actions, it's the other person's positive and encouraging responses that enhance the experience, isn't it?

Of course, many pretend to maintain the illusion. Perhaps that's why nature wisely built self-enjoyment into us—to ensure fulfilment even in solitude.

As in the animal kingdom, some individuals engage in sex mindlessly and casually, primarily those who constantly think about it. Conversely, evolved human beings reserve it for moments of genuine, natural desire, rather than seeking it compulsively.

Be mindful that sex is one of the most powerful intoxicants. The chemicals it releases in your body can lead to irrational actions that you may later recognise as insane and regret. It is also commercialised in various forms, targeting the weak-hearted and exploiting the helpless, ultimately destroying their lives. Indulging in any form of it will eventually erode your sense of responsibility and ruin your happiness.

Conflicts

Persistent conflicts in close relationships, especially with your spouse or partner, can easily ruin your happiness. What may begin as minor disagreements can escalate over time, developing a life of their own. Much of the love gets lost between what is meant, what is said, and what is understood. Eventually, you may find yourself regretting the presence of someone who was once exactly what you desired in your life. It causes damage every day, even if you don't see or interact with the other person, or if you choose to part ways permanently.

Psychologically divorcing your partner is challenging because you still need someone to hold accountable for your mistakes and shortcomings. You may find yourself replaying past conflicts, seeking validation from others about how unfairly you were treated, and even comparing new relationships with your past—often in a negative light.

Without letting go of anger and bitterness, it's impossible to fully move on from a relationship and liberate yourself from its lingering grip.

A close friend of mine, after grieving the loss of his wife to cancer for a couple of years, finally decided to open his heart again. Encouraged by loved ones, he signed up to a matchmaking site, cautiously optimistic about finding someone who shared his values and preferences.

After a few weeks, he came across a profile that resonated with him. She, too, had endured her own struggles—a painful divorce a few years earlier. They exchanged messages, shared pictures, and spoke on the phone a couple of times before deciding to meet for dinner at a cosy, elegant restaurant.

The ambience was romantic—dim lighting, flickering candlelight, and soft music adding to the warmth of the evening. Conversation flowed effortlessly, filled with laughter and a mutual sense of hope.

As the night unfolded, she began speaking about her ex-husband. She had nothing good to say about him—only accounts of disrespect, denial, neglect and violence before he moved on with one of her friends, forcing her to fight a losing battle for justice in the courts.

As they stepped into the cool night air, she suddenly reached for his hand. Holding his gaze, she asked softly,

'Can you help me put him behind bars—even for a day?'

You can adapt to a chronic illness, a major setback, or even personal loss—but conflicts in close relationships are far harder to overcome. For the sake of yourself, your partner, your loved ones, your children, and their children, it's vital to address and resolve such issues consciously. Only love has the power to end hatred.

Unresolved conflicts don't disappear on their own. If buried alive, they tend to resurface later, with greater intensity and in more destructive ways. You've seen how it impacted Anand and Preethi's lives. The tragedy.

Don't ignore early signs such as a significant drop in meaningful conversations, repeatedly bringing up issues without resolving, frequent misunderstandings, arguments over money, unfavorable comparisons with others, constant criticism, belittling one another, or showing disrespect and sarcasm through tone of voice or body language.

Other warning signs include preferring to spend time apart, lack of emotional or physical intimacy, hiding things from each other, feeling unsupported during hard times, and neglecting shared responsibilities.

Recognising these signs early and addressing them through open communication—and counseling, if needed—can prevent the relationship from deteriorating further.

It's quite possible that your partner is fully occupied with work that supports you and the family, but it does not financially. Remember, they still have financial needs, such as buying things for themselves, their parents, children or friends. They might even have to ask you for money to buy a gift for you.

I suggest providing such partners a fixed amount each month for their personal expenses. This will give them freedom and boost their self-esteem and confidence.

It will also help them appreciate the value of money and manage it better. They may even save or invest a portion, which could contribute to family needs or support you in times of need.

Mutual respect is the foundation of good relationships, but for men, in particular, it is essential for proper behaviour and functioning. When men are not respected by their wives or children, it can deplete them and potentially lead to extreme negative behaviours, such as neglect or even violence.

Women, on the other hand, often find it difficult to imagine or engage in such behaviours due to their feminine traits and motherly affection, which may lead them to view even their husband or father as a son.

Therefore, respecting men helps them become better individuals. However, men should be mindful of their own behaviour, especially when respect is lacking because women thrive on love, affection, and emotional connection. They need to feel heard, understood, cared for, and emotionally secure in the relationship in order to truly respect their men. Both partners should consciously break out of this vicious circle to maintain a healthy relationship.

The typical age when couples face severe conflicts and may initiate divorce is often midlife, usually between 40 and 55, as this period tends to bring several significant life stressors.

Women, due to hormonal changes, may become less resilient to stress, more easily irritated, and experience decline in cognitive abilities, task efficiency and emotional or physical intimacy—often pushing their partner to extremes as well.

This stage also often coincides with career and financial pressures, questioning life choices, and seeking new directions for both partners. When combined with children entering their teenage years and even leaving home, it can create a 'perfect storm', making the relationship difficult to manage.

Both partners should be mindful of these challenges and support each other—not just for a few weeks or months, but often for six to eight years or even longer.

As you might have noticed, Anand and Preethi were taking the right steps toward progress and happiness in their early years—but by their mid-forties, they began to behave differently, and their lives started to decline.

Most people face problems in their lives. However, many choose to ignore them or complain without acting to resolve them. They even pretend to be happy—while silently burning out.

The first and most important step in solving any problem is to acknowledge that it exists. The next step is dedicating all your effort and energy to finding solutions.

There are no standardised training programs or frameworks for solving life's problems. Trial and error is often necessary. Read, listen, ask questions and seek help. If one approach isn't working, try something else.

Remind yourself that you don't know everything, and, like any other person, you are also learning, adapting, and doing your best to move forward in life.

Hold hands only with your partner and create a small circle. Don't allow anyone else into it including your parents, children or close friends. By working together closely and constantly, the two of you can find solutions.

If either you or your partner is experiencing any mental health conditions such as attention deficiency, anxiety, depression, etc., take proactive steps to address them. Don't overlook hormone imbalances or vitamin deficiencies. Your relationship should take precedence over what others think, assume, or speculate about your situation.

For your marriage to succeed, you must invest focused effort in learning, growing, innovating, and adapting, similar to what you do in your business, job, or career. This applies to your physical relationship as well. Success cannot happen if your priority and focus lie elsewhere, such as hobbies, job, friends, parents or children. This could mark the beginning of the end of your relationship.

If you decide to end the relationship and start another, finding happiness may be more challenging. Statistics show most second marriages end up in similar situations or even worse. Divorce rates for second marriages exceed 70 percent, compared with about 50 percent for first marriages.

While biological children often act as unifying forces in first marriages, stepchildren often introduce conflict in second marriages.

Unless we undergo a drastic change, we tend to seek a partner with similar dynamics to our previous one in our next relationship because our mental conditioning finds certain traits attractive. This can lead to the recurrence of the same issues.

Many couples later realise that their first marriage wasn't as bad as they thought—or even better than their current one—when they face similar or unexpected challenges in their second.

You may possess both male and female physical traits, and your sexuality may not align with them, making it difficult to identify strictly as male or female. Additionally, you could be homosexual, bisexual, or asexual in terms of sexual orientation.

To maintain long-term and meaningful relationships, it's crucial to approach them with thought and clarity, as many social norms and legal frameworks may not be applicable in such cases.

Your Options

You will encounter many situations in life, but there are essentially only three possible reactions:

You can either accept it, change it, or leave it.

Acceptance means acknowledging the situation, recognising that you may be powerless to change it, or choosing not to invest your efforts in changing it—whatever your reasons may be.

Change means taking responsibility and action to improve the situation for yourself or others. Of course, you may not know whether it would work—but unless you try, how will you ever know?

Leaving it involves recognising your inability to accept or change the situation and choosing to move on.

Take a simple case where you didn't like what was served for dinner today.

You may choose to 'Accept' it if having food in the company of others is more important to you than the dish itself, or if you are very hungry, or any other reason.

If you can't accept it, you can choose to 'Change' it by making something yourself, having someone prepare something for you, or by ordering from a nearby restaurant that matches your taste. It's important to take responsibility for making the change.

If you are unable to accept or change the situation, you may decide to 'Leave,' which means skipping dinner. You do know the health benefits of fasting, right?

Any other reaction—like anger, blaming, complaining, worrying, or resentment, adds no value to you or others. In fact, they often diminish your effectiveness and happiness, as well as that of those around you.

You can apply this approach to any circumstance in your life and see how well it works for you. That's the power of choices.

The ability to change what's important to you is the highest form of freedom, isn't it?

It's crucial not to carry forward the bitterness of these choices into the future. To fully benefit from your wise choices and to experience happiness and joy, you must leave them behind.

That is forgiveness.

Forgiveness is for your own sake, not for others. It's about putting your past behind you and concentrating on the future, releasing your anger, pain, and hurt, and focusing on what is truly important to you.

Let me share with you the story of a snake that crawled over a saw and was injured. As the most venomous creature in the animal kingdom, the snake could not take the incident lightly and became angry.

In its rage, the snake wrapped itself around the saw and began to squeeze it to death. However, with each enraged squeeze, the pain intensified, but the snake was determined not to let the saw escape the suffering it had caused.

The snake struggled for a while, unable to move past the pain and anger it felt, and eventually died.

You punish yourself with anger for someone else's mistake. Buddha aptly compared holding onto anger to 'you consuming poison and expecting the other person to die.'

Not only anger, but also resentment, worry, and negative emotions in general release stress hormones and suppress 'happy' chemicals in your body, making things worse and, if prolonged, leading to various health issues.

Forgiveness requires strength, which can only arise from your awareness and clarity. Weak people seek revenge, the strong forgive, and the wise ignore, refusing to let such matters affect them.

If you are unable to forgive someone, consider the following steps.

Imagine that person's face. Ideally, find a photo and zoom in. Look closely—notice their hair, forehead, eyebrows, eyes, nose, lips, ears, cheeks, chin, and neck. Gaze into their eyes and observe the compulsiveness and helplessness reflected there.

Recognise that people often act out of compulsion—regardless of the conflicts it may ignite, the harm it may cause others, or the risks it may pose to their own future. Appreciate this—not to justify their actions, but to understand their struggle.

Realise that both of you come from the same planet, the same source of creation, share common ancestors, and will ultimately return to the earth when your time comes.

All your negative feelings towards that person will disappear on their last day without any effort on your part—but you may be left with shame and regret for not forgiving them while they were still alive.

You never know whether you'll have the chance to do it tomorrow, and by the day after, that person may no longer be here.

Forgive now.

None of us knows how long we get to live.

Let go of the past. Smile at the person. Feel the relief and joy rising within you. Focus on what matters most to you, and move forward.

There will come a time in their lives when they will regret how they treated you. The same may be true for you. So why wait until then, carrying the burden all the way?

People or their circumstances may not change overnight—or may never change at all. Your life becomes easier, more efficient, and far happier when you can appreciate their struggles, be slow to judge, and quick to forgive.

Step 5

Righteousness

Where there is righteousness, there is success. Righteousness encompasses your responsibility towards yourself, your family, society, and the environment.

What is right and what is wrong?

Is it based on our mental conditioning or the culture we are part of?

In reality, it's often a combination of both, and they are interdependent.

Doing what is right typically leads to positive outcomes, while engaging in wrongdoing tends to have negative consequences.

Laws are often designed to reinforce desirable behaviours and deter undesirable ones, aligning with cultural norms. All these factors ultimately contribute to shaping an individual's mental conditioning.

Now, what about culture? What role does it play?

Culture encompasses the collective beliefs and behaviours of a group of people. It serves as a guide for individuals to behave acceptably to everything and everyone around them and make decisions. However, what's considered right in one culture may be seen as wrong in another.

I recall the real-life story of a young actress that she shared on a popular television channel. It sparked widespread debate on social media platforms as it deeply touched upon the moral code of conduct and value systems within society at large.

Her story unfolded as follows.

Her mother was a homemaker, and her father worked at a private company. Life was going well until everything turned upside down when she lost her father in a road accident at the age of twelve. Life became increasingly challenging, and her mother's lack of education made it difficult for her to find work and support the family.

There was not enough money to cover school expenses, clothes, or even food. Her mother began working as a domestic worker in a household to make ends meet. Later, she took on work in multiple households to support additional needs and provide her daughter with the education she required. Her mother sacrificed a lot, working long hours from early morning to late evening.

She grew into a graceful young woman, graduated from a reputable college with a degree in the performing arts, and developed a passion for acting. She started her career in television series and also landed roles in a few films. Although she was unable to earn much, she and her mother managed to live comfortably.

Her mother was her entire world until she got married. She married a handsome man from the same industry and also had a six-year-old son when this incident occurred.

Her mother then fell seriously ill (she did not specify the illness) and was hospitalized for several weeks. She and her husband borrowed money from friends and family, in addition to spending all of their savings, to pay for treatment. However, her mother's condition worsened, and she was referred to a super-speciality hospital for further treatment. The family didn't have enough money to clear the hospital expenses or cover the costs of transferring her to the new hospital.

Despite raising some additional funds from friends and family, they still fell short. Time was running out, and they couldn't find any other financial resources to save her mother.

At that point, she contacted a couple of dating agencies, informing them that she was willing to accompany anyone to earn some money. The agencies attempted to contact their regular customers, but no one was available on such short notice, and some even requested appointments for the weekend. Although she waited for a few days, nothing worked out, and her mother passed away.

She broke down multiple times while recounting her story, pausing to compose herself. Her pain, shame, and guilt moved many viewers deeply, sparking widespread discussions on social media.

Five years had passed since the incident, and her son was now eleven years old when she shared her story. On the programme, she offered heartfelt apologies to her husband, son, mother-in-law, extended family, friends, and anyone else she could think of, pleading for forgiveness. It was clear that she was enduring far more than she was able to express.

The topic sparked debates on most social media platforms the following day.

It went on like this.

'How could she even consider that—no matter how desperate the situation is?'

'Hey, it is a classic example of true love and immense sacrifice.'

'If she was forced into it, we'd all be standing by her, right?'

'If she were unmarried, maybe it would have been understandable. But she is a wife and a mother!'

'She should have asked her husband for permission.'

'Would she be okay if her husband had done something similar?'

'It was not cheating—it was an act in exchange for compensation.'

'Should not humanity take precedence over morality in such situations?'

'Since it did not happen in the end, there is no real issue.'

'No, no. What runs through the mind is more significant than physical actions.'

'Even if it had happened, it would not have changed her love for her husband or son. So, what is really wrong with it?'

'It was inappropriate for her to reveal it now—and that too so publicly. It is bound to hurt her husband, her son, and the entire family.'

'She ought to be tried in court for infidelity.'

'Not needed. Her own guilt and shame will haunt her more than any punishment ever could.'

And so on…

Righteousness

What is right remains right, even if no one practises it. What is wrong remains wrong, even if everyone is doing it. This applies to everything, from something as small as carelessly stepping on a snail to something as serious as taking someone's life in self-defense.

Life often puts us in situations where we struggle to decide what is right and what is wrong. Sometimes, telling a lie might be tempting for a better outcome, but it poses a significant moral dilemma.

Cultural and legal norms regarding right and wrong may not provide definitive guidance, since they are often specific to particular groups rather than universal truths.

According to the Karma philosophy, your actions are considered right if they are performed without selfish motives such as money, power, fame, reputation, or even favors, but rather for the greater good of others.

From this perspective, it advises against actions such as:

Not keeping your word, breaking promises, taking back what you have given, regretting your gifts, or discouraging others from giving.

Stealing or taking away someone's livelihood or possessions—especially from women or children.

Getting overly attached to sensory pleasures.

Earning money through deception, not repaying debts or misusing entrusted deposits.

Focusing on others' faults while ignoring their virtues, or hating what is good.

Slandering good people, envying those with merit, dishonouring parents or teachers.

Cutting down large trees, gardens, or forests, destroying wells, ponds, tanks, shrines or homes, and obstructing public paths.

Taking pleasure in conflict, or making and selling weapons meant to harm others.

Being cruel to other beings, consuming intoxicants, or being lustful toward someone else's spouse.

Destroying an embryo, neglecting your spouse, children, or those who serve you.

Showing unkindness to the weak, giving false testimony or punishing the innocent.

Being ungrateful, betraying friends, ending relationships, or destroying others' hopes.

Whether you prefer the scientific view or Karma philosophy, this advice can guide you to live your life as an evolved human being. They encourage upholding righteousness, embracing grace, and finding happiness and joy in life.

I hope there are no areas where you may be doing wrong. However, if there are, becoming aware of them is the first step toward making the necessary changes to put things right.

According to the Karma philosophy, 'One can digest even iron filings, but not something that belongs to someone else.' This implies that even if your ancestors, parents, or others committed wrongful actions and you are benefiting from them, you are still considered to be in the wrong.

Once you become aware of such wrongs, it becomes your responsibility to take corrective steps to the best of your ability.

If you are seeking direction or deeper insight, the scriptures of any religion can offer valuable guidance. The concepts and characters they present serve as timeless, tested examples for people from all walks of life.

At their core, all religions share three key aspects: values, symbols, and customs. While values remain consistent across all religions, it is only the symbols and customs that vary.

Yato Dharma Tato Jaya in Sanskrit, which means 'where there is righteousness, there is success', is the underlying message of all religions and scriptures.

Righteousness encompasses your responsibility towards yourself, your family, society, and the environment. It is about fostering an intimate connection with everything—living or nonliving—around you, encouraging you to dedicate sincere efforts to making the world a better place for everyone. These are the hallmarks of spirituality.

War is one of the most devastating events that can occur in any civilised society, often marked by brutality and destruction, driven by motives of power, wealth, or both. Throughout history, there has never been a good war or a bad peace. However, if a war is deemed necessary for the greater good, it must be governed by a code of conduct.

The Kurukshetra War, chronicled in the Indian epic, the Mahabharata, which dates back several thousand years, is a prime example of this concept.

Each day, the battle would cease at sunset, allowing hostilities to subside, and even the warriors would mingle freely as friends. Single combat was to occur only between equals, with horsemen were permitted to engage only other horsemen, but not foot soldiers. Similarly, elephant troops and chariots were restricted to attacking only their counterparts on the enemy side.

It was deemed inappropriate to attack individuals who were unarmed, without armour, retreating, surrendering or even distracted. Non-combatants, such as those blowing conches or beating drums, were also off-limits as targets.

As we have discussed, Karna, the great warrior, was attacked and killed while he was unarmed, with his attention focused on lifting his chariot wheel stuck in the ground. Krishna clearly explains why Karna, despite his prowess as a warrior, did not deserve fair treatment because of his numerous wrongdoings, which even instigated the war itself.

Doing what is right is the most important thing, no matter who you are, where you are or what you do.

Your Biggest Ally

Having explored your responsibilities towards yourself, your loved ones, and society, it is now time to reflect on your responsibility towards the environment.

Mother Earth has generously supported you from the beginning of your life journey to who you are today, and will continue to support you until your last breath.

Have you been kind, courteous and grateful to her?

In 1960, 62 percent of the wilderness remained untouched. By 1997, it had dwindled to 47 percent, and by 2020, only 35 percent remained—reduced by almost half in such a short span of time, and the decline continues.

We have been fishing more each year while also polluting the ocean, which is our largest and most vital farmland. At this rate, the sea may soon contain more rubbish and plastic than fish.

No fish contaminates the water. No animal erodes the soil. No bird pollutes the air. Yet we, as humans, contaminate every element we come into contact with—air, water, and soil. We have waged war against everything beautiful on this planet, inflicting pain and stifling the joy of life.

And yet, amidst all this, Mother Earth continues to give—quietly, generously, and without expectation.

Let us consider the coconut tree. The white kernel inside the coconut is used in everything from everyday meals to gourmet delicacies. The shell is made into beautiful handicrafts, and the coir from its outer husk is used in carpets, cushions and mattresses. Its leaves are used for thatching roofs and making brooms, while the trunk provides strong, durable wood for building. Additionally, tender coconut water serves as an energy drink, and the syrup extracted from its flower is packed with nutrition.

Can you think of any human who contributes to others in so many different ways?

Creation has endowed every living being—whether a worm, insect, ant, fish, bird, animal, or any other life form—with the necessary capabilities to survive and thrive. There is no reason to believe that we are more significant than any other species or that we hold special rights over them, or over the planet.

If all the worms and insects were to perish, all other life on the planet, including us, would soon follow suit. On the other hand, if all humans disappeared, the planet would flourish. Trees would break through rooftops, and birds, butterflies, and snakes would reclaim the spaces we once occupied. Within just a few years, these places would transform into lush forests filled with all kinds of life—except us.

We make up only 1 percent of all living beings on Earth, yet we are the most dominant species. No one can stop us—except ourselves.

Mother Earth, like your mother, is incredibly generous. Given the chance, she will gladly and abundantly restore all that we have damaged. Supporting her is much like caring for your mother's health and happiness, and expressing genuine gratitude.

Yes, protecting the environment is part of the Constitution in several countries, either as a fundamental duty or a constitutional right.

Since the global economy is precariously dependent on consumerism, it does not just appreciate when you buy what you truly need but everything you are influenced to buy for business growth and profits.

Take the clothing industry, for example. By promoting excess as fashion and trends, garment production has increased rapidly over the past few decades—far beyond what people actually need.

The fertilizers and pesticides used in cotton cultivation, along with the toxic chemicals used in bleaching and dyeing, pollute the soil, water, and air indiscriminately. The clothing industry is now the second largest industrial consumer of water and the second-largest contributor to global carbon emissions—right after the oil industry.

As fashion trends shift or after only a few uses, these garments are discarded and end up in landfills, placing a greater burden on the environment.

Think twice before buying new clothes. Many people shop because of boredom or to spark a little excitement.

See whether you can still wear your old clothes at home, or donate them if you no longer wish to. Your rubbish could be someone else's treasure.

If they're no longer wearable, use them as cleaning clothes in the kitchen or around the house. When they are completely worn out, consider giving them to repair and maintenance workers who always find such materials useful.

It is not just about clothing—but everything you buy, use, and discard. Buy only what you truly need and use it to its fullest.

It goes beyond purchases to how you use resources.

Choose public transport over private vehicles, and walk or cycle short distances instead of relying on motorised transport.

Avoid using air conditioners or heaters unless absolutely necessary, and make the most of natural light to reduce electricity use.

Say no to single-use plastics; carry your own cloth bags, bottles, and containers.

Harvest rainwater and consider installing rooftop solar panels to generate your own electricity—and even contribute any surplus to the grid.

Support recycling and repurposing whenever possible—every small effort counts.

These are just a few simple actions that are not only nature-friendly but also beneficial for your well-being and wallet. Of course, there are many more along the same lines that you can think of and practise.

Take a glance at any landscape painting. Typical scenes depict majestic mountains, a sunrise or sunset, lush, green trees, a winding stream, or a flowing river. In the valley below, you'll often find small houses, grazing cows, blooming gardens, fluttering butterflies, birds soaring high in the blue sky, and children playing joyfully in the park. Everything in the painting mirrors the natural world.

Everything that humans have created—whether it's buildings, bridges, cameras, microphones, robots, airplanes, air conditioners, artificial intelligence, or anything else—has been inspired by nature. Everything in nature is operating with immense beauty and phenomenal intelligence. Nature is not only your strongest ally but also your greatest inspiration.

Your attention, creativity, compassion, tolerance, and both physical and mental health all thrive when you are attuned to nature and also nurture it.

It may not always be easy or comfortable to be nature-friendly, but it's our responsibility—and essential for our survival and well-being. This isn't just for ourselves, but for our children, their children, and generations to come.

Step 6

Excellence

The value of your life is defined by your contribution to others, not by your educational level or the type of work you do.

Every living creature on the planet works—whether it's an ant, elephant, plant or person. For most species, work is essential for survival, but for human beings, it goes beyond that, particularly after a certain point in life.

Your happiness in life is deeply influenced by how you feel about your work. Whether you're a homemaker, freelancer, working in an organisation, running your own business or engaged in any other role, you work to meet your needs or fulfil your desires.

I'm not quite sure what people mean by work–life balance. Is your work and your life truly separate?

Not really.

It's all one—your life!

If you see them as different, it's not your life. So most of the concepts and techniques we explore here apply to your workplace, home, and even other settings.

Your work will occupy a significant portion of your life. The other major activity that takes up your time is sleep—essential for recharging your body and mind for the next day's work.

Dissatisfaction at work inevitably spills over into your personal life—and vice versa. Home and work continuously influence each other, for better or worse. There's no need to emphasise this further—the good and bad aspects of it in Anand's and Preethi's lives remain vivid and searing in our minds.

Your work can serve as a job (for income), a career (focused on growth, goals and recognition), or a calling (driven by purpose and service to the greater good). Whatever the category, you're engaging in activities that carry meaning for you at that stage in your life.

Have you ever considered what you would do if you weren't being paid? Imagine how happy you could be if that passion became your job or career!

Whether you're a homemaker, teacher, farmer, doctor, mechanic, artist, lawyer, engineer or engaged in any other profession, the true value of your work lies in improving the lives of others. Likewise, someone else performs those roles to support your own life. So, do your work well, as it serves not only your own needs and desires but also those of others.

India's Constitution, under Article 51(A), recognises excellence as a fundamental duty of every citizen: 'to strive towards excellence in all spheres of individual and collective activity so that the nation constantly rises to higher levels of endeavour and achievement'—emphasising both personal effort and teamwork.

It's a privilege to make a positive impact on someone's life. Don't hesitate to step forward and offer help if it can benefit someone, even if success isn't always guaranteed. Ultimately, the value of your life is measured by your contribution to others, not by your level of education or the kind of work you do.

Education

Education is one of the most important aspects of your life. Much of your formative years are spent learning, gaining knowledge and developing skills. Whether through formal schooling or informal experiences, education forms the foundation of your success.

Studying subjects such as language, science, maths, history, and geography at school serves several purposes. It helps you understand the world around you, use this knowledge in your daily life, contemplate your interests, and recognise the additional knowledge needed to pursue what matters to you. Education isn't just about earning a living; it's about enriching your life.

Learn anything with the intention of applying it in real life, ensuring thorough understanding. Simply accumulating multiple university degrees or even a PhD doesn't guarantee clarity or competence in performing a job well; they may only indicate the volume of information acquired.

Accumulating knowledge without a clear purpose or practical skills to use it can become compulsive or even addictive. It can dull your ability to listen, dampen your curiosity and stifle the joy of life.

In India, small tea shops are found everywhere, offering hot tea and snacks. Particularly in villages, they serve as popular hangout spots, even if you're not in the mood for tea. People gather here to discuss various topics, and these conversations often continue long after the tea is finished.

It's common to see notices such as 'Do not discuss politics here' on shop walls to prevent heated arguments.

By listening to and participating in conversations, the shop owner gathers much information. This enables him to form opinions and provide suggestions on various matters, such as what the finance minister should do to reduce the fiscal deficit, what the football team needs to fix to win the next national league, why currency devaluation is beneficial in the current situation, what the space organisation should focus on as the next big thing and why investing in gold is a good decision now.

Of course, he won't have the skills to apply them. And more importantly, that information won't help him brew good tea. If your education turns out the same—a lot of knowledge but short on skills—it won't serve its real purpose for you or anyone else.

'You should learn well' is something you start hearing about from childhood, is it not?

How do you actually learn well?

When learning anything, it's crucial to invest extra effort in grasping its nuances, exploring new perspectives and extracting valuable insights. The ability to apply these insights effectively in life is what constitutes wisdom. I agree that as a student, there's often less motivation to do so, given that most exams prioritise memory recall over insightful understanding.

Additionally, you're likely to forget what you've learned quickly if not applied. It is often observed that after reading a book, hearing an insightful message, or watching a meaningful video, it can be difficult to recall them after a while, let alone apply them meaningfully.

One effective method for addressing this issue is by taking notes on key points and your insights as you engage with information, whether you're reading, watching, or listening. It's best to do this electronically for easy retrieval later on.

Over time, these notes will accumulate, effectively building a personalised encyclopedia. Though it may lack the structure of a book, there's value in that as well.

When you search for something, you'll likely come across additional information that has been forgotten. This process helps refresh your memory and encourages you to consider topics from fresh perspectives. These unintentional revisions can further enhance your insights and increase the likelihood of applying them in your life.

As a student, until about the age of twenty-five, you focus solely on learning and honing your skills to excel in your chosen path for the future. It's important not to get distracted during this crucial period by politics, romantic relationships, intoxicants, or anything else that doesn't contribute to your primary goal. There will be plenty of time for such pursuits in the future. Trust me.

Schools may not teach rocket science, but they can nurture your imagination to soar beyond the clouds. Anything that prompts you to think and imagine represents true education. Ensure you also allocate ample time in solitude, away from distractions, to tap into the power of your independent thinking.

As often noted during college reunions, the quiet student may emerge as a successful businessman, the below-average student may excel as the most awarded army officer, the athlete may transition into a successful coach, and the disengaged student may rise to become a CEO.

Yes, your success relies on both your imagination and your intelligence.

The term 'intelligence' originates from the Latin word 'inter-legere,' meaning 'to read between the lines.' While intelligence is undoubtedly a valuable capability, it remains constrained by the lines above and below or by the limitations set by existing knowledge.

However, it equips you with the ability to connect the dots and perceive things that others may overlook or fail to comprehend. Yet, it may also lead to boredom with tasks that don't demand much intellectual effort.

In contrast, your imagination has no bounds compared to the limitations of your intelligence.

It was when I was specialising in computer software after my engineering. Our professor asked us to come to the networks lab after class because one of the computers was connected to the internet. It was among the first locations in the country to have an internet connection in those days.

He told us he could send an email to his friend in the United States and receive an instant reply. I was surprised, curious, and struggling to understand how this was possible, as at the time, mail existed only in paper form and was delivered through postal services.

As the professor demonstrated it in the lab, I imagined he would insert a paper message into a slot in the computer and receive a printed reply from the same slot immediately. It may sound amusing now, but please pardon my ignorance.

Instead, he typed a message on the screen:

'Are you there?' and pressed Enter.

An immediate reply appeared on the screen:

'Hi there, how are you?'

It took me some time to comprehend because I had never experienced anything like that in my life.

I would imagine the people who invented the internet also faced similar limitations in their intelligence, but they were able to imagine beyond them.

Intelligence often makes things larger and more complex. The touch of imagination is needed to make them simple and intuitive.

In addition to your studies, ensure you participate in activities such as sports, arts, crafts, debates, and more. Engaging in these activities helps tune all your learning channels to acquire wisdom. They also foster discipline, coordination, focus, and perseverance—essential qualities for success in life. Neglecting these pursuits may lead to rigidity and limit personal growth, hindering your overall growth and development.

In ancient times, the *Gurukul* education system in India was structured around these principles. Students stayed with the teacher to ensure their studies remained unaffected by their home environment.

They lived together, rising early to play and study until noon. In the afternoon, they participated in tasks such as cleaning, gardening, gathering firewood and other essentials from the forest, and helping in the kitchen, thereby enhancing their life skills.

The curriculum aimed to make them healthier, happier, stronger, and wiser, instilling respect and reverence for everything around them. The ultimate aim and measure of success was to cultivate knowledgeable, skilled, fearless, and humble individuals.

Contemporary research also finds that children who engage in daily household chores from an early age are more likely to develop better discipline, greater confidence, higher self-esteem, and are more likely to succeed and live fulfilling lives.

The original goal of commerce was human well-being, but in recent years, this goal has been compromised for the sake of economic growth. Educated individuals have commercialised nearly everything for profit, including education, healthcare, well-being, sports, spirituality, and even sex.

Merit is often overshadowed by wealth, as those with money can gain entry into prestigious universities and careers such as engineering, medicine, or law. This devalues merit, effort, and performance, leading such individuals to seek shortcuts in everything. They might work in places where the relentless pursuit of profit compromises both the quality of work and human values.

If your education encourages ego, excessive pride, injustice, cruelty, jealousy, greed, and selfishness, then you are not truly educated as these traits often stem from ignorance.

Instead of producing educated brutes or skilled manipulators whose selfish interests cause tragedy for many, education should foster compassion and encourage people to contribute to the well-being of others, especially those who lack similar opportunities in life.

I hope everyone, including students, teachers, parents, and professionals, will reflect seriously on this message.

Four Types of Work

There are millions of jobs, but only four fundamental types of work exist, and they've been around since the beginning of time. These are Educators, Warriors, Merchants, and Labourers.

Throughout your lifetime, you might engage in a few of them or all of them in cycles, or even simultaneously. It's essential to embody their characteristics to be effective and happy while performing them.

Educators share their knowledge through various means such as teaching, training, coaching, counseling, research, literature, religion, spirituality, and more.

Warriors protect the lives and property of others by participating in the military, police force, justice system, social activism, and various political systems.

Merchants engage in profit-driven business through sales or investments. They offer goods or services that benefit others.

Labourers form the largest community and primarily view their work as a means to earn their livelihood, enabling them to support themselves and their loved ones. This category encompasses a wide range of occupations including homemakers, engineers, mechanics, doctors, nurses, technicians, private investigators, farmers, carpenters, plumbers, accountants, artists, and athletes, among others.

Consider the example of a doctor and an auto mechanic, both fall under the category of labourers and undergo rigorous training and skill development for their respective jobs. While a doctor diagnoses and heals various parts of the human body, such as the brain, heart, lungs, digestive and excretory systems, a mechanic inspects and repairs vehicle components like the computer, engine, air circulation, fuel systems, and exhaust units.

Both professionals utilise similar tools for diagnostics, analysis, and observations. Additionally, while blood and bodily fluids may stain a doctor's hands and coat, mechanics often encounter oil and lubricants in a similar manner.

The patient's life could be lost if the doctor makes a serious error. Similarly, if the mechanic makes a mistake, the lives of the driver, passengers, and even the people around could be lost.

Mechanics cannot repair their bodies on their own, and doctors cannot repair their cars by themselves. Both are dependent on each other to carry out their lives.

Which job is more critical? Who should be paid more?

Every job is important because if it's not done well, severe consequences can result. A job may seem easy to someone who isn't doing it because the challenges faced by those in the field are often invisible to those outside of it.

While compensation is influenced by supply and demand like anything else in the market, it's crucial to provide good working conditions to enable everyone to perform their job effectively.

As you know, all your organs are equally important for your well-being because an impaired colon can affect even how your brain functions. Similarly, even if everything else is working well in your vehicle, if the tyre is not fixed properly, it could be your last drive. It would be ridiculous to rank one job above or below the other.

A practicing physician is a laborer, but a teacher of medical science is an educator. A warrior is someone who takes up missions like making essential medical care affordable, even in remote villages. A merchant is someone who operates a healthcare enterprise for profit.

Although your medical knowledge may be helpful, each category requires a different version of oneself to be successful in those roles.

In other words, based on what matters to you at any particular stage of your life, you may choose to take up the right role(s) leveraging your knowledge and skills. The financial gain across these categories may also vary, where educators often earn much less than merchants and even laborers.

Running an education, healthcare, or legal support business purely for profit; focusing on sales or business development as an engineer—with increased networking and travel while spending less time with your family; or fighting in a war not to defend your loved ones or country, but for political or economic gains—may not align with the true nature of the job and what truly matters to you.

These situations may lead to internal conflict, detachment from your work, and job dissatisfaction. Your success and happiness here depend on your clarity and conviction.

Path of Excellence

Great job! Well done!

Isn't that what everyone wants to hear at the end?

Even feedback like 'you could have done better' can disappoint you, right?

Yes, that is the fundamental construct of every human being: to do good and feel good.

Regardless of whether compensation is monetary or otherwise for your work, you should always strive to do your best if you've accepted the responsibility. When you don't do everything you can, you let down the people who depend on you.

Whether you're making rubber slippers or rocket engines, collaborate with everyone and everything involved to achieve the best outcomes. That is true professionalism.

What sets professionals apart from amateurs is simple: professionals work to benefit others, whereas amateurs often focus on doing what they enjoy.

Waiting for rewards or status to perform well can hinder you because it is typically not how recognition is earned. The rewards will come in some form if you perform your duties well. At a minimum, improved work-related skills, efficiency, and reputation are valuable rewards in themselves, which you can capitalise on anywhere you go.

Excelling as an engineer doesn't automatically make you a good manager. To succeed in management, you need the aptitude and skills to lead and support others. Without these abilities, both your time and the efforts of those relying on you may be wasted. It's crucial to develop these skills on the job and pursue excellence to earn recognition and status—not the reverse.

Low-quality output and rework lead to a significant waste of human effort, resulting in multiple costs for individuals, employers, and the environment. Additionally, it compels individuals to spend excessive time at work to complete tasks, leaving them with little opportunity to learn and develop skills for their current job and future opportunities. This perpetual cycle can lead to mediocrity, dissatisfaction at work, and a constant sense of unhappiness.

When I worked for a well-known multinational corporation, the Business Unit Head (BU Head) occasionally visited my team, as he did with most other teams in the business unit. He seemed to have ample free time as he would spend a significant amount of time chatting with the team during his visits.

These conversations rarely revolved around work; instead, they focused on topics like the recent cricket match, the latest movie releases, new restaurants he had tried, sensational news, or jokes.

Most of the team members would gather around him, eagerly joining the conversations, agreeing with whatever he said, and even laughing exaggeratedly at his jokes. Ironically, I didn't see many of them show comparable engagement in their work tasks. After the visit, some senior members would even accompany him for extended discussions at the coffee shop.

Just a handful of team members, fewer than 10 percent, never participated in these discussions and would often resume their tasks immediately after a quick handshake with him. Interestingly, these individuals were also among the best in their field. One such employee was busy taking measurements and recording them in his workbook when the BU head noticed him.

Before heading to the coffee shop, the BU head approached the employee and inquired about what he was doing. The employee, visibly enthusiastic, briefly explained his task, provided an overview of its development status, outlined the competitive landscape, emphasised its significance in the upcoming product release, and highlighted its benefits for customers.

Soon after, the BU head shifted the conversation to other topics, asking about the recent cricket match and a movie, but the employee admitted he wasn't up to date on them. He redirected his attention to the measurements he had noted. Observing the employee's disinterest, the BU head changed tack and inquired.

What are your future plans? The employee simply smiled in response.

Curious, the BU head pressed further, asking, 'Where do you see yourself in five years?' The employee responded with a cold stare.

Undeterred, the BU head remarked, 'You seem indifferent to these topics, yet you appear incredibly happy and enthusiastic. I ought to learn from you.'

'What's your secret, young man?'

The employee replied politely, 'I have a lot of work to do, sir.'

Clarity about what truly matters to you is the driving force here.

As discussed, even if you are clear about your desires, it's possible that you're currently engaged in activities to meet your immediate needs until you acquire the skills and abilities to pursue them. The best way to handle this phase is by doing your present job very well.

Does that sound contradictory?

It isn't—because by doing your job well and reducing rework, you optimise your time and effort at work, freeing up more time to educate yourself and acquire the skills and abilities necessary to fulfill your other needs and desires.

Your most important job every day is to be better than you were yesterday.

As you know, although Anand wasn't initially working in the biomedical equipment field—his true passion, driven by a desire to provide critical medical care to villages—he stayed focused, honed his skills, excelled in his job, and made steady progress in meeting his needs. At the same time, he kept developing relevant skills on the side, eventually transitioned into his dream job and thrived. You may also recall how his life declined during the later stage of his career when he was no longer able to work in the same way.

Clarity helps you envision your future, make decisions without delay, prepare well, find enjoyment in your work, and advance both professionally and financially in your current job. Joyful individuals tend to progress faster because they are more likely to commit to tasks, embrace learning opportunities, acquire new skills, excel at work, increase their earnings, and move forward with their plans.

Without clarity, even with continuous external incentives, it will be difficult to achieve even minimal performance.

Performance = Potential − Internal interference (due to lack of clarity)

You will be at your best when you are able to utilise your full potential. Your superior performance in anything you do will primarily depend on the accuracy of your self-assessment.

Clarity leads to faster, efficient, effective and joyful action. I call it C x A.

Clarity will set you apart from the majority. It will compel you to use your time and effort effectively, instead of wasting it as others often do, allowing you to focus on learning, honing skills, and excelling in everything you do. Of course, you must be willing to live differently from others to do so. Remember, it is not necessary to know everything. Focus on what truly matters to you and delegate or outsource everything else whenever possible.

Very few people actually work a full 8-hour day, despite claiming 10 to 12-hour days. The typical average is only 4 to 6 hours. Seems too little, doesn't it?

You should aim to put focused attention and effort into accomplishing more than this to complete your tasks on time amidst the distractions of irrelevant emails, unproductive meetings, interruptions, social media, and personal tasks that fill a typical workday.

Avoid accepting every meeting invitation or responding to every email or message unless your input is truly valuable. The sender should justify your participation.

This does not mean maximising every minute. It also involves taking time to appreciate the beauty of everyday moments—pausing to reflect, enjoying a casual conversation over coffee, listening to your favorite music, sharing a meal with family, or simply enjoying the small things throughout the day. Allocating this time won't happen on its own; you have to plan for it too.

Though humans have a more evolved and capable brain, it still cannot truly multitask. While they can handle basic multitasking like walking and talking, they are incapable of processing attention-rich inputs simultaneously. The brain cannot allocate equal and adequate attention to a lecture, presentation, and conversation simultaneously. Since these tasks engage a significant part of your brain, you can't effectively focus, filter out irrelevancy, and extract valuable insights.

Undivided attention is the key to effective learning and mastery. This will push your cognitive capabilities to their limit, improve your skills, and create new values that are hard to replicate.

Connect with others to understand their perspectives and insights and foster meaningful collaborations. When you talk, you are repeating what you know, but when you listen, you may learn something new.

When you hear anything new, you'll try to fit it into what you already know, which can make listening difficult. Acknowledge what you do not know, ask questions, no matter how simple they may seem, and seek help when required. Remember, every expert was once a beginner.

A mentor can be an invaluable resource if you seek specific knowledge or skills. Meeting them in person isn't always necessary; you can gain insights from their books, workshops, or teachings. However, if you want to gain from their guidance to advance your career or business, you need to actively involve them.

It's a reciprocal relationship where clarity about your goals and what you can offer your mentor in return strengthens the relationship's impact.

Excellence and happiness are the outcomes of sacrifice, hard work, resilience in the face of failure, patience, and passion, whether in the realms of education, work, arts, sports, marriage, or anything in life.

Overcoming personal obstacles such as ego, excessive pride, envy, greed, selfishness, lust, anger, and fear is crucial, as these traits can hinder progress by narrowing your vision, distorting your perspective, corrupting your values, and leading to manipulation. Therefore, work hard on yourself before you work hard on anything else.

While brilliance and talent are essential, they alone cannot produce results without discipline and commitment. Discipline entails forgoing immediate pleasures for greater rewards in the future.

The majority—constituting 90 percent, may often be critical, sarcastic, and unsupportive towards you because they lack your knowledge, your perspective, and your aspirations. It's important to avoid giving anyone the impression that you consider yourself superior to them, as this can hinder effective collaboration. Even if they don't have a positive relationship with each other, they may still unite against you.

To achieve your goals, you'll need support from superiors, subordinates, and peers. Resistance from others is inevitable in any path you choose in life. Whether someone supports you willingly or not, it's challenging to force cooperation, even with positional authority.

When you hold a position of power, people may show you gestures of goodwill throughout the day, such as greeting you frequently, opening doors for you, spending time with you, paying undivided attention, agreeing with whatever you say, offering you a seat, or offering tea or coffee in a special cup.

However, these actions are often motivated by your position, not genuine regard for you as an individual. The same treatment would likely be extended to whoever occupies that position.

Once you no longer hold that position, people may not treat you in the same special manner, except for those you've helped, supported, or positively impacted. It's essential not to be swayed by such treatment or feel disheartened if you're treated differently. What truly matters is your character, commitment, and competence (the 3Cs), shown through discipline, courage, integrity, support, respect, trust, patience, and excellence.

You naturally assist others in achieving success as you reflect success and fulfillment in your own life. As more people look to you for guidance and support, you'll continue to grow and expand, receiving their support in return because people want to help those who help them. Even without formal authority or a title, you can still guide and lead by example. As a true leader, embodying personal excellence combined with teamwork.

Leadership often dismantles existing structures and systems to create new ones for efficiency and effectiveness, whereas authority is about maintaining existing systems and hierarchies, inhibiting change.

Being a good leader also means being a good follower. It enables you to collaborate effectively with other leaders and support their plans and programmes, thereby enhancing overall efficiency and effectiveness.

Leadership involves partnership, cooperation, mentoring, and support. If you don't walk a few steps with someone, you can never guide them in a different direction. It demands significant effort, commitment, and sacrifice.

Teamwork

In most situations, we work in teams, even at home. Working in teams enables us to share ourselves meaningfully with others and leverage their skills and resources to achieve common goals. Everything we do in such a setting is expected to have a much greater impact as a group than it would individually.

Working in a team is vastly different from working alone, as the results depend on the abilities and efforts of everyone involved. Despite the potential for greater results, many people prefer to work alone, as teamwork necessitates adjusting, adapting, changing preferences, collaboration, and coordination.

Teamwork is a valuable skill that requires development and nurturing. It requires changes in both what you do and how you do it, and it involves letting go of individualistic tendencies learned from childhood in favor of a collaborative mindset. This holds true even when working with just one person—your life partner—as we discussed earlier.

When collaborating with others and leveraging their strengths, you'll inevitably encounter their weaknesses as well. Any strength, when inadequate or excessive, can manifest as a weakness. Asking individuals to develop may delay results, as it might take them some time to reach the desired level. Furthermore, they may not be inclined to do so if it doesn't align with their needs, desires, and plans.

Invest in their strengths and position yourself and others to compensate for their weaknesses. Ensure your teams have a broad mix of strengths so they can complement one another and achieve their goals. If improving those areas is essential for meeting their needs and desires, they may choose to do so. Allow them to handle it independently and at their own pace; it's their life, after all.

Even if their development may not directly impact short or medium-term shared goals, genuinely support them in their growth. The best way to help them is to foster self-discovery and skill building to focus on what truly matters to them.

Take full responsibility and encourage others to do the same in pursuit of common goals. Holding people accountable isn't disrespectful or unreasonable; it demonstrates your belief in their capabilities and your commitment to the task.

Excuses such as 'somebody broke it,' 'somebody needs to fix it,' 'I don't know how to do it,' and 'it's not my job' won't lead to results. Instead, take ownership and find solutions.

Response-ability is the capacity to choose your response to maximise your own and others' potential in an interdependent environment, leading to great results. This mindset demonstrates a positive attitude.

Clarity of purpose is essential for any decision or action you take. Whether you're considering furthering your education, switching jobs, changing your children's school, making special arrangements for your parents, adjusting your plans or schedule, or any other matter, articulating the 'Why,' 'What,' and 'How' is crucial.

These details should be clearly stated and agreed upon by all parties involved to achieve the desired velocity and efficiency in execution. This is leadership—setting the vision and creating positive pressure. Whether on the basketball court or the battlefield, once the team understands the rationale and strategy, they will execute it effectively.

Consider Anand's objective when he was developing the portable dialysis device:

Why:

To make a significant difference in the lives of individuals who were forced to expend considerable time, effort, and financial resources traveling from remote villages to urban centers for critical medical care.

What:

A low-cost portable dialysis machine enables patients to conveniently undergo dialysis treatment from the comfort of their own homes, eliminating the need for frequent travel.

How:

The machine, with the ability to perform dialysis, can upload medical reports, enabling remote access for doctors to prescribe treatments online. It's available for purchase for those who can afford it or with an accessible rental option for others.

The 'Why' is the most significant aspect. When the 'why' is clear and meaningful, both you and those around you become excited, energised, and committed to making it happen, especially if it resonates with one's life's purpose. Many ideas will emerge for the 'what' and numerous possibilities for the 'how.'

Asking additional 'whys' helps develop more clarity. Each subsequent answer enhances your understanding and its significance to you.

Why 2:

Travelling twice weekly to urban centres for dialysis consumes a significant portion of their remaining lifespan, spent on bus or train journeys, which worsens their already fragile health.

Why 3:

The frequent travel to cities prevents both the patients and those accompanying them from working, thereby significantly impacting their livelihoods.

To achieve your goals, every member of your team is crucial, extending beyond those you closely work with. Many others indirectly contribute to your work and life, including those who maintain your workplace's functionality and safety, manage cleaning and prepare meals, to mention a few. Never look down on anyone. You also need not look up to anyone, as you have the same potential and opportunities as everyone else.

When someone goes missing, the public, police, rescue teams, and even the armed forces join the search, utilizing all available resources to locate and save that person. Nobody considers age, gender, social status, education, or knowledge to judge the importance of the missing person or to measure the rescue efforts because every individual is important. The same holds true in similar situations, such as bus or train accidents, flight crashes, floods, earthquakes, or other natural calamities.

Avoid ranking people according to their importance to you. Treat everyone with respect and value their contributions. Whether it's the doctor or the nurse, both are essential to your recovery. Recognizing the importance of each individual helps them feel valued and motivated to give their best effort. After all, everyone's deepest desire is to feel valued and recognised.

In the Indian epic, the Ramayana, there's a story where Lord Sri Ram praises a small squirrel for its contributions to a monumental project. Sri Ram and a large team was working tirelessly on building a bridge across the Indian Ocean from Rameswaram, situated at the southernmost tip of India, to wage war in Sri Lanka.

Amidst labourers carrying heavy stones from the mountains and placing them into the sea to build the bridge, there was a tiny squirrel. It was carrying small pebbles and sand, dropping them on top of the stones in the sea. Although its contribution may seem insignificant compared to others carrying heavy stones, it gave its best, doing all it could, without expecting anything in return.

Lord Sri Ram was so moved by the squirrel's sincere efforts that he ran his tender fingers over its back in gratitude and admiration.

This story highlights the dignity of labour, the significance of selfless participation and teamwork, and how even a small contribution can be significant when one gives their best effort.

'As a squirrel, whatever I can' is a well-known phrase in India, often used in such contexts even today.

Small and gentle also have their strengths.

Workplace Culture

Workplace culture refers to the collective beliefs and behaviours of individuals within a specific workplace.

I have experienced considerably different work cultures among American, Canadian, Chinese, German, Israeli, and Indian teams—and again, noticeable variations across the government, private, and startup organisations I've worked with. I also created an open, informal, disciplined, and high-performing subculture within my project teams, which received multiple awards for best teams, projects, products, and businesses.

In addition to your clarity on what matters to you and the knowledge and skills you possess to excel in your job, your workplace culture should also support and encourage high performance.

This implies selecting a workplace aligned with your values, needs, and goals. However, if circumstances prevent you from selecting your ideal workplace, you should operate effectively within that setting to excel in your role. No excuses.

What is a good workplace?

Given the diverse backgrounds, beliefs, and values of its members, a healthy workplace should promote mutual respect and trust, facilitate effective decision-making, and enable efficient collaboration toward common goals. It should also provide the freedom to realise your potential, pursue your needs and desires, and be your authentic self. If any of these aspects are compromised, you're unlikely to find happiness in your work.

I recall a case study of a major American multinational corporation that prided itself on reporting a higher diversity ratio, particularly in terms of women in leadership positions and on its board of directors. This milestone was widely praised, especially considering the challenges women face in male-dominated industries. However, when reviewed by an independent agency, the results were surprising.

To compete in these positions traditionally held by men, many of these women had to adopt more masculine traits over time. Unfortunately, in many cases, this came at the cost of suppressing their feminine qualities, negatively impacting their relationships and personal lives.

Businesses solely focused on branding and profits may lack the intention and expertise to support, guide and ground the individuals in such scenarios. As a result, the expected diversity and inclusion goals remained unmet, and the desired outcomes were not achieved.

Let us not celebrate gender, but who we are.

Women often excel at internalizing responsibilities and executing their duties proficiently. They take care of their families, maintain household order, fulfill social obligations, and undertake many other tasks often putting others before themselves.

They typically work quietly, focused, tirelessly, and anonymously, often without seeking rewards or recognition. Their motivation isn't necessarily driven by personal preference; rather, they do what needs to be done out of a deep sense of commitment and professionalism.

Indeed, women who work full-time, balancing both their domestic and professional responsibilities, face significant challenges. However, they often experience lower levels of stress, fatigue, and health issues compared to men, and they also report greater happiness and well-being.

Men often take on roles as protectors and providers, while women embrace nurturing responsibilities, driven by their respective masculine and feminine traits. Families, communities, and institutions thrive when these diverse strengths are united creating a strong partnership built on teamwork and mutual support.

Three Types of People

Success in any workplace hinges on fostering positive working relationships with co-workers, stakeholders, and customers. Ongoing conflicts with any of these parties can significantly impede your effectiveness, efficiency, and overall happiness in the workplace.

In any workplace, you'll encounter three types of people: those who actively 'Support' your efforts, those who passively 'Allow' you to proceed, and those who actively 'Hinder' you, impeding your progress.

Their behavior is influenced more by their capabilities, life experiences, beliefs, and values than by who you are and what you are doing, although workplace culture can play a role in moderating their actions.

Those who actively support you are invaluable assets. Keep them informed of progress and changes, actively engage with them, and consider their opinions and feedback. It's essential to nurture these relationships to ensure their continued support.

Those who merely allow you to proceed are neutral observers. While you shouldn't rely on them to take direct action, it's beneficial to keep them informed about plans and progress. In the long run, this transparency may lead them to actively support you. More importantly, it can prevent them from hindering you in the future.

You might find it challenging to deal with individuals who hinder your work. However, it's essential not to prejudge someone based on limited knowledge of their life story. Approaching them with an open mind is advisable, but investing excessive time and effort to align and gain their support may not be fruitful.

Instead, keep them informed of your developments through newsletters, blog posts, or general emails. Over time, these may gradually encourage them to shift into the category of those who allow you to proceed.

Many individuals exhaust themselves trying to win over this group, leading to unnecessary conflicts and draining their time, energy, enthusiasm, and happiness. It's crucial to avoid falling into this trap.

The Art of Saying 'No'

To prioritise and focus on what's important to you, it's crucial to master the art of saying 'No' effectively. In various situations, whether at work or elsewhere, you may be asked to undertake tasks that you're unable or unwilling to do. This could be because you feel it is not aligned with your priorities or skills, or you do not have the time for it.

In such cases, if you cannot accommodate the request, your only option is to decline politely. However, it's also important to navigate the situation delicately to minimise potential conflicts.

Two key strategies can make your 'No' more acceptable.

Firstly, ensure that your refusal stems from clarity rather than being a reaction to who made the request.

Secondly, provide a brief explanation to help the other person understand your position. Additionally, offering an alternative solution can further ease the situation.

For example: 'I won't be able to take on this task until Thursday, as I'm tied up with an event and other pending tasks. I can share the document that I currently have. It should be easy for you to modify it to suit your needs. Please let me know if you have any questions, and I'll be happy to help.'

Even if you can't change your circumstances, you can control how you respond to them. Balancing your focus and goals with respect, empathy, and compassion is crucial, as it impacts not only your well-being but also those around you. How much someone likes you depends on how they feel in your presence. Being liked opens doors to new opportunities and enhances your effectiveness.

Effective Communication

Effective communication is essential for achieving efficiency and effectiveness in any workplace. It not only conveys information but also resonates emotionally, blending facts with dreams, emotions, humility, and humanity.

If you think your communication did not reach your audience, make the necessary changes and try again. Over-communication is not bad because if it was well received the first time, the recipient will simply ignore it the next time. It's much better than missing the message, right? Crafting a strong subject line is crucial to capture attention and facilitate future searching.

For example:

Subject: Our Green Corridor solution has begun saving lives!

Hello Team,

As you're aware, 30 percent of lives are lost due to delayed medical assistance. I'm thrilled to share that our solution, which switches traffic lights green as ambulances and emergency vehicles approach a traffic junction, has been deployed in multiple cities and has begun saving lives. Great job!

Thank you for your perseverance and for making it happen despite numerous challenges.

Let's continue to strive towards deploying this solution across the country and beyond.

Best regards, Your Name

Ensure written communication is clear and concise to achieve the targeted outcome without the need for further questions or clarifications.

For example:

Sub: Action Required: Mandatory Training for New Accounting Software

Hello all,

We are introducing new accounting software next month. Mandatory training sessions will be held on May 10 and 11 from 9:00 a.m. to 12:00 p.m. in the training room 108. Please sign up by April 25 using the link below.

Note: Online attendance will not be available. If you cannot attend the training on either of these dates, please discuss it with your supervisor promptly.

Signup link:

Thank you, Your Name

Just like written communication, verbal communication also deserves careful attention to be truly effective. Talking has become a compulsive behaviour for many, driven by reasons such as fear of being ignored, showcasing knowledge or superiority, seeking validation, fear of being seen as weak by staying quiet, wanting attention and control, or simply discomfort with silence.

Being clear and mindful about why you speak, what you wish to convey, and how you say it can save time and effort—for both you and those around you.

Loud and continuous talking can make it hard for others to follow what you are saying. Good conversations involve well-timed pauses, allowing for meaningful exchanges. When others fail to pay attention to or appreciate your words, it's often best to remain silent.

Avoid using foul language, as it is disrespectful, and diminishes your value not only in the workplace but in any setting. You will be more refined and effective without it.

Thank people and share credit. Listen attentively, acknowledge others' perspectives, and ask questions humbly, all with a smile. Encourage passionate debates, as long as they are conducted with respect and kindness. This fosters an open, direct, and friendly atmosphere where everyone can perform at their best. However, this doesn't equate to softness, which can be unreliable and easily influenced.

I have even used theatre as a powerful medium of communication within my teams—an approach that was later adopted across the organisation—to raise awareness and sensitise employees on topics such as innovation, teamwork, performance, discipline, ethics, and harassment.

Even after making a careful choice, it's possible that the work you do or the workplace culture may not align with your needs, desires, or values. In such cases, it's okay to move on if you're unable to accept or change them. Remember, you're not a tree rooted in one spot—you have the freedom to adapt, grow, and flourish elsewhere.

Fear and Failure

'Failure is the stepping stone to success,' 'If you succeed you lead, if you fail you guide,' 'Failure is your best teacher,' and many more. That is easier said than done.

Most people pursue education to find a well-paid job that meets their needs. Later, once these needs are met, their desires become more significant. However, if they cannot pursue them, it becomes a major source of unhappiness.

Regrettably, they will not risk losing their good salary, title, or status at their current job, nor will they take a break to learn new skills and pursue their desires.

Their expensive purchases, which don't keep them happy for long, according to the adaptation principle previously discussed, will force them to stay at their current job to pay back their loans, compounding their unhappiness.

They may complain about boredom, fatigue, and frustration at work but often don't take definitive steps to change because they are accustomed to complacency, conformity, and the ordinary.

It reminds me of how monkey catchers trap monkeys. They go to places where there are monkeys and begin eating groundnuts in front of them. They don't give groundnuts to the monkeys but leave a handful in small holes they have made in the trunks of trees. These holes are such that the monkeys can insert their hands into them, but they are not large enough to withdraw a hand filled with groundnuts. A very simple design!

The catchers then go and hide at a distance. The monkeys come out and try to get the groundnuts from the holes in the tree trunks. Their hands, filled with groundnuts, get stuck in those holes, and the catchers come over and catch them.

Of course, the monkeys have the option to leave the groundnuts and run away to freedom, as their open hands can easily come out of the holes. Instead, they are caught because they don't want to let go of what they have—driven by craving and attachment.

The fear of failure is a major obstacle to leaving what you have and pursuing what you want. It is the enemy of personal growth. This, in one way or another, can prevent you from fulfilling your desires.

Stability and excellence often lead to monotony and stagnation. You may find yourself as an expert, comfortable, or possibly underperforming.

Regularly reflect on when you last learned something new and consider if change is needed. Embracing change brings new surroundings, new people, excitement, challenges, learning, and growth.

Some stress is beneficial for performing well because the human brain thrives on challenges, but within an optimal zone of difficulty. Easier tasks may lead to boredom, while overly difficult ones can result in frustration and giving up. Education, knowledge, and skills should expand your possibilities, not promote comfort and risk aversion. Make growth the daily sport you play to celebrate life.

I'm not implying that you're unaware of these things. People are born with self-respect, dignity, enthusiasm, curiosity, motivation, and joy in learning. Unfortunately, we often erode these qualities one by one, starting from our schooling years, where emphasis is placed on marks, grades, and rankings, even for extracurricular activities.

Becoming a scientist does not necessarily require exceptional intelligence, superior memory, or top grades in school; what's essential is a deep-seated interest in science.

The modern education system does not operate in that manner due to the diverse interests of commercial institutions, parents, teachers, and even students themselves. It tends to produce a steady stream of similarly skilled and like-minded individuals to cater to the predominant job markets by delivering information uniformly and through standardised mediums. In this system, teachers primarily speak while students passively listen, resembling a factory assembly line.

Few positive qualities that remain after your education may gradually be dismantled in the workplace as you become part of the so-called 'performance management' system that rewards top performers and punishes those at the bottom. This fosters unhealthy competition and undermines team efforts, resulting in outcomes far below individual and group potential.

The emphasis on rewards and recognition for completing tasks at any cost, as ordered by the boss, instills fear and greed, and mirrors the dynamics of the schooling system you are familiar with.

What is fear?

Fear is something that intimidates you and convinces you it's a threat. Overcoming it takes determination and focused effort.

Usually, when we're afraid of something, we avoid it—right? But can you stop sleeping just because you're scared of nightmares?

So, do the opposite. Afraid of being on stage? Get on stage more often. Scared of traveling? Make it a point to travel. If you fear relationships, work on building healthier ones.

Everyone has fears. What truly matters is how you face them and rise above them.

In my childhood, we used to go to the nearby river to play and swim. We'd spend hours there, often losing track of time, prompting our parents to come looking for us. Each day, the water level and currents in the river would change due to rainfall elsewhere, so we'd assess the conditions upon arrival to decide what to do.

One day, we underestimated the flow and drifted while attempting to swim across the river. I found myself in a deep area. Exhausted, I sank several times and swallowed a lot of water. The water had a blue hue there. Crossing that area took a tremendous effort, and I barely avoided drowning. I was about ten years old at the time.

After that incident, I was terrified of entering the water, especially if it was blue. My parents and family circle cautioned me that overcoming my fear would take time, but they gently encouraged me to get back into water. I started by walking in the shallow water, gradually regaining the courage to swim, even in deeper areas with a blue hue.

It took a couple of years to conquer my phobia, but eventually, I fell in love with the water again. To this day, swimming remains one of my favorite activities.

What is failure?

Failure can be defined as the inability to achieve an expected outcome, whether it is gaining something new or maintaining what you already possess. It doesn't depend on one's knowledge, skills, wealth, social status, or circumstances but rather on one's expectations, typically in comparison to others' achievements.

Regardless of what you have, compared to another person, you might perceive it as less, sufficient, or more and also feel happy or unhappy about it. This comparison can involve your parents, siblings, classmates, friends, co-workers, neighbours, or anyone else. Rivalry driven by jealousy, in fact, is one of the main reasons for issues in families and close relationships.

The process of striving to become somebody is often the root cause of human suffering. It can be painful to try to be anything other than yourself. There will always be someone further ahead than you—someone with more education, a better job, a bigger house, a nicer car, more money, a prettier partner, better-behaved children, or better circumstances.

One moment, it tells you that you are great, and the next moment, it tells you that you are the worst. Either way, it blinds you to your true self and what truly matters to you.

If your goal is to surpass someone, you may experience temporary happiness upon achieving it. However, soon after, you'll set a new goal based on someone else's achievements, which can lead to unhappiness until you reach it. This cycle can limit you, as you may be capable of achieving much more than any of them.

As you may have observed, if you perceive yourself as either far superior or inferior to someone, there is little room for competition or jealousy towards them, right?

We exist in a vast universe, with millions of galaxies, each containing millions of stars. Among them, the sun is just one such star, and Earth is one of the planets orbiting it. We won't survive if the sun doesn't shine or the earth's rotation slows down or stops, even for a moment.

Here on Earth, we have many nations, billions of people, diverse terrains, expansive seas, numerous wonders, including a vast array of living organisms. Humans comprise only 1 percent of all living beings and are akin to any other natural resource.

As astronauts observe from space, Earth appears as a tiny blue dot, with no national boundaries or any sense of orientation like east, west, up, or down, and humans do not even register as a speck. Despite being such a micro speck in the middle of nowhere, feeling successful and happy simply because you believe you are one step ahead of someone else in your friends, family, or social circles, in your locality, or somewhere on this planet is not success—it is a sickness.

This may manifest as shame in pursuing certain actions—even if they are the best course of action at the time—such as closing your unprofitable business, accepting a job that doesn't require all your educational qualifications or offers a lower salary than your previous job, seeking treatment for your mental health, continuing or ending a difficult relationship, or even something as simple as choosing to disengage with someone because you believe they are not the right fit for you.

Can you recall the last two embarrassing things you have done? You might worry that others still remember them. Conversely, can you remember the last two embarrassing things someone else did? Chances are, you can't recall any because, rather than remembering them, you have better things to do in life, right?

The same applies to others. They aren't thinking about you in the way you might think they are. They're not dwelling on your accomplishments or lack thereof; they're busy with their own lives, not yours. So, instead of worrying about what others may think, focus on moving forward and living your life fully.

Even lions, the kings of the jungle, only succeed in 25 percent of their hunts, meaning that 75 percent of their attempts are unsuccessful. Similarly, most plant seeds never get the chance to sprout, and half of fish eggs are consumed by other creatures. It takes more than a million flower visits by a honeybee colony to produce only 500 grams of honey, which we often take away, thereby disrupting their plans.

Despite these low success rates, none of them give up on their endeavors. That's the law of nature. Only humans tend to view a few unsuccessful attempts as failure, often because success is measured against someone else's achievements.

Most technological advances and conveniences unconsciously train us for instant gratification. With the click of a button, we can stream movies, shop, bank, prepare food, and adjust the temperature of our surroundings. Motorbikes, cars, trains, and flights allow faster travel, while computer networks enable instant communication over text, voice, and video with anyone and anywhere.

However, even a minor interruption or decline in their performance can leave us feeling upset, angry, and stressed. It's important to remember that nothing in nature operates at such speed, except calamities.

Over nine months in the mother's womb, the pain and wonder of entering the outside world, struggling to turn over, crawling on the floor and skinning your knees, standing up and falling down countless times before taking those first steps, shifting from liquid to solid food, potty training, schooling, employment, marriage, and children—and so much more.

The struggle continues until your last breath. None of it can be skipped or rushed, and no one else can do it for you. If you try, you'll only end up disappointed and frustrated.

Achieving anything positive in your life requires focused attention, sustained efforts, and great care. Even though you might not realise it, patience means having patience with yourself, not others. Your life can be happy and joyful just by being patient.

Let me encourage you to start vegetable gardening, even if it's in a small area like your backyard, balcony, or terrace. You could also consider joining a community farm but aim to contribute as much as possible on your own.

You will witness the journey of a seed as it grows into a plant, flowers, and fruits and eventually produces the next generation of seeds. Animals, birds, or insects can sometimes destroy your crops and undo your hard work. Initially, you may feel disappointed by such occurrences, but they will soon become part of the process.

This will improve your patience and tolerance for uncertainty, give you more hope, and better prepare you for failure. Consequently, you will learn how to invest your effort while also accepting that results are beyond your control.

Karmanye Vadhikaraste Ma Phaleshu Kadachana in Sanskrit means 'perform your duty without being attached to its results.' If you constantly focus on 'what's in it for me,' you may attain only trivial gains. However, when you let go of this mindset and focus on your work, being deeply involved and without fear of failure, great accomplishments can follow.

This teaching, imparted by Lord Krishna to the great warrior Arjuna on the battlefield of Kurukshetra, is one of the profound lessons of the Bhagavad Gita. There are no failures in life, only results.

Comparing and competing with others are the biggest distractions and can stifle your imagination and creativity. They rarely lead to extraordinary achievements. Your happiest and most fulfilled self emerges when you pursue what truly matters to you, without comparison to others. Your destiny is unique, and there is no competition for it—each one has their own.

Consider the scenario of Ramanujan, the Indian mathematician who proved several new theorems before the age of 22. He did poorly in most of his subjects in secondary school and worked as a clerk at the Chennai seaport in Southern India after completing his education. Remarkably gifted in mathematics despite lacking formal training in the subject, Ramanujan was later invited to Cambridge in England, where he made significant contributions that surpassed many well-known mathematicians.

Now, imagine if he were still alive today and part of your family, friends, professional or social circle.

Do you wish to compete against him, follow his path to success, or seek his support to pursue what matters most to you?

He may not be able to assist you with anything beyond mathematics because there's nothing remarkable about him apart from his mathematical prowess. Even in mathematics, what worked for Ramanujan might not work for you, considering he claimed the formulas came to him in dreams, inspired by his family's Goddess.

If you have the sickness of feeling happy when you possess something others lack, you might take a photo with him and share it with those who haven't had that opportunity yet. What matters to you most has nothing to do with Ramanujam, though.

Even if you are clear-headed, have your own benchmark for success, are competent, dedicated, and give your best effort, things may not turn out as you hoped. Even if highly successful individuals in your family, friends, professional, or social circles are willing to assist you, what worked or works for them may not produce similar results for you.

The outcomes depend on numerous factors that you may not be able to imagine, fully comprehend, plan for, or control. In scientific terminology, repeating the same action in the same manner can yield different results because outcomes are typically not deterministic, but probabilistic, influenced by various external factors.

Most geniuses, great leaders, multimillionaires, well-known figures, and history-makers have experienced setbacks and rejection at some point in their lives, whether they be artists, sportspeople, professionals, technologists, or entrepreneurs. Kings, queens, and even the gods of any religion we worship today were not spared from such experiences. It's highly unlikely that you could be an exception.

As you cannot prevent others from facing difficulties—whether a growth crisis, illness, or challenges at school or work—you cannot expect more from others when you go through similar situations. The best someone can do is offer support while you navigate your struggles—certainly not with insensitive advice like 'relax' or 'take it easy.' It may be hard to handle initially, but as your faith grows stronger than your fears, you will find it easier to cope.

Cheerful faces don't necessarily mean that those individuals are free from problems; rather, they often possess the ability to handle them. Those who have faced adversity and setbacks often develop greater strength, compassion, tolerance, fulfillment, and resilience.

These experiences have also equipped them to face problems better than others who have never encountered such challenges. They push you to surpass your beliefs and limitations, unlocking your potential to grow as a high performer, leader, and human being.

When you are desperate, you become more attentive, innovative, and focused on overcoming challenges. Your strength comes from your focus and clarity rather than your intelligence. It's similar to how we study more effectively the day or two before a test than when we have ample time during regular study periods.

You can take currency of any denomination. It possesses intrinsic value and the potential to acquire anything in exchange for that value. Its worth does not change whether it has been used before, misused, soiled, kept in a nice wallet, or whether it's in an urban or rural setting. The same principle applies to your worth as well.

Like most people, you too would have been attacked, knocked down, kicked, mistreated, or misused. You would also have experienced betrayal from people you trusted, injuries from those you loved, and devastation from events you could never have imagined. However, none of these experiences can diminish your value, who you are, or what you can become. Your worth shouldn't be determined by whether you are liked, respected, or treated nicely.

You've become the person you are today as a result of all the difficulties you've overcome, the toxic people you've encountered, and the trials you've endured. You are much more powerful now than you may think.

If you're not feeling great right now, it's possible that you're a little tired. Rest if needed, but don't give up on your future before living it. If you give up, it's guaranteed that it will never happen in your life; otherwise, there's a possibility.

Learning from mistakes may sound simple, but it's not always easy. Still, it's essential before trying again.

We often avoid sitting down and addressing what makes us fail. Instead, we try to blame reasons such as 'it's not my area of expertise,' 'at my age, it's hard,' or 'the market is not ready for it.' We need to be brutally honest with ourselves to introspect and figure out what we are doing wrong, whether the reasons are small, significant, or obvious.

It's essential to address them honestly, make changes in weaker areas, adjust the course slightly, or take a completely new perspective when trying again. Breakthroughs often come from consistent prior efforts that build up the potential to unleash significant results.

Alexander Fleming, the inventor of penicillin, once remarked that its discovery was an accident. He observed that a fungus formation had killed the strain of bacteria he cultured. Curious, he re-cultured the bacteria, tested it with the fungus again, and realised it might hold promise as a solution for bacterial infections. This led to the development of the life-saving medicine, penicillin.

Such breakthroughs often go unnoticed without a breadth of experience, clarity, focus, and a willingness to inquire, all of which don't happen by accident.

Your intuition and curiosity are powerful internal compasses. Follow them and pursue what truly matters to you, by loving what you do.

'Dreams are not what you see in your sleep, but those that don't let you sleep', said Dr. A.P.J. Abdul Kalam, who rose from humble beginnings to become a renowned scientist and the Missile Man of India. He served as my program director during my time in Defence Research and Development, and later became the President of India.

Others may tell you that you can't achieve your dreams because they couldn't achieve theirs. Don't let those who have given up on their dreams discourage you from pursuing yours. Distance yourself so their voices no longer affect you. Listen to your inner voice above all others.

Retirement

Schools, college, assignments, exams, grades, marks, tests, job interviews, work, promotions, job changes, and more—it's all behind you now. It's time to step away from what you've been doing for quite some time. You may start contemplating how to earn a living, how to spend your time, and what new things you want to begin.

Of course, you will eventually move on from them as well. Starting with the work you've been engaged in for a long time, you will gradually retire from various activities as you move forward.

If you had worked diligently, taken care of your health, and maintained good financial discipline, it's quite possible you would have met most of your needs and some of your desires before retirement, achieving financial stability, even if you started with a low-paying job at a young age. On the other hand, even with a high-paying job, you could still be far from financial stability and may need to continue working for money.

Someone who earns a few thousand can be in more debt than someone who earns only a few hundred, and this is often the case. It doesn't depend on how much you earn, but on how well you manage your finances, without worrying about others' opinions.

If you have expertise to offer, you will be in demand. Older individuals typically experience less job stress, lower absenteeism, make wiser decisions, and have higher productivity than younger counterparts. Of course, it's essential to stay healthy in order to perform your job effectively.

Don't dwell on your past—the places you've worked, the positions you've held, and so on. What matters now is what you can offer to those around you and how well you can help others do their jobs effectively.

If your needs are met, this could be the time to pursue your desires. Remember, age is just a number—it does not define your needs, desires, or plans. Your life before fifty is nothing but a warm-up. Even at sixty, you have more than one-third of your life left. The good old days are right now.

If you have fulfilled your desires too, you are free to do whatever you want. You could assist those who are less fortunate than you without thinking about yourself. Charity is more than just giving money or things away. It involves giving your time, focus, and energy to others, as you would for loved ones. You could end up working harder than ever before, without receiving a paycheck, but you will be rewarded in many other ways that will bring you happiness and joy.

Weekends were precious because they were a break from a long week of work. Holidays were exciting because they took you away from your regular routine. But after retirement, when every day can feel like a weekend or a holiday, their meaning and appeal may diminish—even the sweetness of lazy Sunday mornings can wear off when it is no longer rare. That's why it becomes even more important to engage in meaningful pursuits.

Ageing is a beautiful process that helps you become the person you always ought to have been. You don't have to impress anyone anymore. No one expects you to rush around or do things faster, and you won't be frustrated with speed limits or slow-moving traffic.

No one is likely to harm or harass you. As long as you are not required to accompany your spouse, you don't care where they go. Remember, your financial freedom is crucial to your independence because it grants you access to various services through the power of your wallet.

Don't be ashamed of the aches, pains, and ailments that come with aging. Studies show that happiness often increases with age, even in the face of health challenges.

Continue doing physical exercises to maintain muscle strength and body flexibility. To slow down cognitive decline, mental stimulation is just as important as physical exercise. Therefore, never stop learning. Continue to engage in your household and social activities. They will help you remain mentally and physically agile.

Keep your old friends close, but also make some new ones while you're at it. Your happiness is greatly influenced by the relationships you have with your friends, family, and the wider community.

However, learn to enjoy your own company because you may start losing loved ones, including your parents and even your spouse as you age. The younger generation may struggle to spend time with you, as they are busy with their own lives.

Grandparenting can be exhausting in later years but also incredibly rewarding because of the unconditional love you feel for your grandchildren, sometimes even more than you did for your own children. However, don't become too preoccupied with responsibilities towards them or even your own children.

Avoid mocking the younger generation; you've been one before, so you understand how it feels. Instead, encourage them and give them priority because they are just starting out and have a long way to go.

Refrain from assuming wisdom on your end and getting involved in their issues, but offer help if requested. Be a responsible elder and keep your sense of humor, especially about yourself. Your appeal as you get older lies in your health, sensuality, warmth, compassion, and loving smiles.

It was snowing heavily as I walked back home after purchasing everything I needed for the week from the nearby supermarket. I didn't have a car in those days. Struggling with the weight of three bags, my frozen hands and fingers throbbed with pain. That's when an old lady, pushing her bicycle, approached me.

With a loving smile, she asked, 'Shall I help you carry your bags?' I hesitated, yet she insisted.

She suggested I place all the bags in the bicycle's basket. Reluctantly, I placed two bags in the basket and still carried the other one with me. Despite the freezing cold and her struggle to push the bicycle, she accompanied me, taking a detour to carry my things until my doorstep.

As she prepared to leave, she kindly said, 'It is very cold, stay warm and take care, dear.'

Enjoy your leisure time and enjoy the many benefits available to senior citizens. You've earned it. Be grateful to have lived through an extraordinary time in history and to have reached places you had never even imagined.

The best is yet to come—believe it.

Step 7

Gratitude

You are not the sole cause of your success. Be grateful to everyone and everything—living, departed, or even the inanimate objects—for shaping who you are and what you have today.

Isn't gratitude simple, obvious, and natural?

Yes—with a little awareness and practice.

Do we really need to talk about it?

Yes—because gratitude is a key pillar of happiness, yet it's often overlooked.

It's a practice that positively affects your health, relationships, resilience, and overall wellbeing. Through gratitude, you begin to feel that you already have enough, and it helps you cope better during difficult times, build trust and mutual respect, strengthen relationships, and bring lasting happiness.

Yet, despite its power and benefits, why is practising gratitude still challenging?

As we've discussed, human beings possess a remarkable ability to adapt—even to chronic illness. This adaptability helps reduce suffering from setbacks—but paradoxically, it can also become a major source of human frustration and dissatisfaction. What a curious contradiction!

It can compel you to adjust to your successes and reduce your happiness soon until you achieve something new. You may begin to take your achievements for granted and lose your sense of gratitude for them.

If you always desire more than what you have, how can you sustain your happiness and be joyful?

Your happiness = What you have ÷ What you want

If the denominator is larger, your happiness will be less, even if the numerator is huge.

When you are healthy, you may have many needs, but when you are ill, you have only one—to be healthy, right?

Remember, the life you're living now—even if you're not entirely happy with it—is still the dream of millions around the world.

Be grateful to your parents, who gave you the chance to begin a new life and may have sacrificed their own needs and desires for your sake. They might have even postponed buying a decent pair of footwear for themselves just to cater to some of your whims and fancies.

Appreciate your siblings, aunts, uncles and many others who helped you eat, grow, walk, and heal. Thank the teachers who guided you through language, science, mathematics, history, and other subjects, without whom you would not have understood most of what we have explored together.

Gratitude

Be grateful to those who offered you work to meet your needs or fulfill your desires, your colleagues who helped you perform, your friends who supported you in times of need, your spouse who joined you to enrich your life, your children who became a part of your journey, and many more.

Be grateful to the farmers who cultivate crops to provide your food, and to the plants that sacrifice their lives for your well-being. Appreciate the people who work tirelessly behind the scenes to ensure you have network connectivity, running water and electricity, food on your plate, and many other necessities.

Even inanimate objects like your house, furniture, appliances, utensils, car, bike, workbench, and tools quietly support you through each day.

Take a moment to consider something as simple as your dining table—the one that has supported, and continues to support, your family gatherings every day. Perhaps it has been with you since childhood, surrounded by your parents, grandparents, and siblings, and today with your children and maybe even grandchildren. It might be the only place where three or four generations come together to converse, laugh, and share.

It has quietly stood through countless celebrations, cake cuttings, simple meals, grand feasts, homework sessions, casual chats, and deep conversations—not just for you, but for many you hold dear. Be grateful for this silent companion.

Be grateful to everyone and everything—living, departed, or even inanimate—for shaping who you are and what you have today.

With time, this practice will become second nature, helping you appreciate everything you encounter as all of it supports your life in some way. This will nurture humility, realising that you are not the sole cause of your success. This practice can significantly enhance your happiness but also inspires you to give back for what you have received and continue to receive.

Be grateful for what you don't have as well.

Yes, for not being physically or mentally disabled, not battling a serious illness, not suffering from chronic pain, not living in a war zone, or facing earthquakes, hurricanes, floods, or other natural disasters.

Be thankful that you're not alone, not searching for lost loved ones or witnessing their suffering, not subjected to abuse, not bankrupt or homeless, and not enduring prolonged hunger. Extend your gratitude for the many hardships you've been spared.

Be grateful that you are not among the millions who didn't wake up this morning, and for being able to sit in peace and read this book—to pursue what truly matters to you and to live the rest of your life joyfully.

With deep gratitude for everything and everyone, let us now turn to life's final chapter—and gently embrace the reality of death.

Death

While facing death, you realise the life you feared as a snake was merely a piece of rope with which you could have performed some magic.

People rarely engage in conversations about death, often because they haven't experienced it themselves or haven't contemplated their own mortality. For many, the topic evokes fear or discomfort. However, avoiding discussions about death is not helpful, as it is an integral part of life.

Indeed, understanding death can open up possibilities and enrich your life. Since that is our sole intention, let us proceed and explore some of the concepts we've discussed from the perspective of death as well.

If you are afraid, take my hand. Let's head there together.

What is death?

A person is considered to have died when the physical body ceases to function—whether due to old age, illness, or any other cause. The body grows, ages, deteriorates, and dies just like any other living thing on the planet. That is the law of nature. Nothing is permanent, and no one is immortal.

Life is a limited-time opportunity to accomplish what truly matters to you. Time cannot be stopped, rewound, or fast-forwarded, and its experience is relative.

Time flies when you're happy and enjoying what you're doing. Conversely, days may feel longer when you're unhappy, with each minute stretching into what seems like an hour.

Ultimately, when your time is up, you must leave. There will be no discussions, disagreements, or extensions of time. It is absolutely non-negotiable.

You will have to depart alone, leaving behind your body, mind, names, status, wealth, family, friends, and everything you have gathered up until now. People's feelings towards you—whether hatred or friendship—will also die, as they are tied to your body and mind, which will no longer exist.

People who didn't have time to meet or talk to you before will now spend a lot of time visiting your body and talking about you. They will remember your virtues and may even regret that you did not live longer. Yet no one—not even your closest friends or family—can take your place on your behalf, even if you offered everything you owned in exchange.

Those who never gave you a single flower during your lifetime will place a bouquet upon you in death. Your loved ones will kiss your cold forehead, even if the last time they kissed you was many years or even decades earlier. You will be honoured with the same reverence as on the day you were born.

However, the tears will dry within hours. Those gathered will soon begin planning their meals once the funeral concludes.

Over coffee, family and friends will begin to converse. Most of them will soon return to their homes and workplaces, and even your children will leave within a few days.

If you were employed, your colleagues will not seek you the following day, and your employer will begin searching for a replacement.

A few people unaware of your passing will call you one final time, only to be informed by someone else. Your absence from social media may go entirely unnoticed. Within a week or two, your spouse may return to watching regular TV shows and enjoy them as usual.

Of the hundreds you once knew—family, friends, and community—only a few will remember you in the years to come. You will be forgotten far more quickly than you think. I hope you haven't neglected anything truly important in your life for the sake of these people.

Your life requires the support and involvement of yourself and many others, but your death requires nothing from anyone, not even you. It will unfold smoothly and efficiently.

Such is the simplicity—and the quiet beauty—of death.

Regrets in Life

Natural death is not a one-day event but a gradual process unfolding over several months. During this time, all your expectations, pride, inhibitions, embarrassments, and fear of failure will wither away, leaving behind only what truly matters to you: the YOU!

It is then that you realise the life you feared as a snake was merely a piece of rope with which you could have performed some magic.

When confronted with death, most people harbour regrets about their lives. These regrets are not about wealth, status, power, or fame, but about how they missed out on happiness.

- About how they let opportunities pass them by because they were afraid to step out of their comfort zone.

- How they lived lives dictated by others' expectations, suppressed their emotions to maintain peace, and pretended to be happy.

- How they failed to use their gifts and talents, missing the chance to pursue what was most meaningful to them and impactful to others.

- How they missed spending time with their parents, friends, and family, and missed their children's childhood, and their partner's companionship.

Within my family, among my friends, and across my social circle, I've always tried to visit those who positively influenced my life, during their final days.

On this occasion, it was my friend's uncle. He is no longer with us. Despite his outward success, he did not appear to carry that same air during our final meeting. He was unusually vocal and expressive. We spoke for a while, and here's a brief summary of what he shared.

'My childhood was truly wonderful. My father held a stable government job, and we lived in a spacious house. Surrounded by a loving family and supportive friends, I carry many cherished memories. I excelled in my studies and earned a degree in Economics. In fact, all four of us siblings pursued higher education.

After graduation, I secured a lucrative job, relocated to another city, got married, purchased an expensive car, and bought a large home. Over the years, my wealth, status, and reputation soared, but unfortunately, time with my family and relationships dwindled as I became increasingly busy.

After a few years on the job, every day at work began to feel the same. Dull to begin with, followed by the usual routine and a predictable end. There was nothing particularly exciting to mention—just grey, not vivid. Of course, I received many awards and accolades at work and was considered highly successful by my family, professional, and social circles,' he added with a regretful chuckle.

'I wanted to start a microfinance company to provide simple and quicker loans to farmers and small businesses, but I always postponed it out of fear of losing my secure job and status. Additionally, because we didn't have a business background, my family circles discouraged it as well. I didn't realise how much courage was needed to fully live my life.'

'After finishing their studies, the children left home to focus on their jobs, families, and children. My father passed away first. I regret cutting short his funeral rites to just five days as I had to return to work—like many other family members. My mother then stayed with me. I realised how deeply I missed my parents. She brought meaning to my life for a while, but she too passed away a couple of years later.'

'I believe my body has aged faster than the years I've lived. The busy lifestyle caused many ailments and my health to collapse before I even realised it. The only support I have now is from my wife, who has taken care of everything and everyone since we were young.'

To hold back his tears, he gazed out the window.

'I've devoted the majority of my wealth, which I've worked my entire life, to charitable causes. I came to realise that pursuing wealth beyond what I really needed did not make any meaningful difference for me. Sadly, this realisation came too late. I shouldn't have waited so long to give more to those in need. Those happy faces would have added greater meaning to my life. As for my micro-finance company, I don't know how it would have worked out, but I didn't even try.'

I could sense he was going through far more than he was sharing. It reminded me of the lemon-and-spoon race—where you win not only by walking faster, but by balancing the spoon and, more importantly, by not dropping the lemon.

'Hey, young man, you shouldn't live a life like this. Follow your heart, enjoy every step, and create something meaningful,' he said, raising his voice a bit, which shook me out of my thoughts.

This isn't an isolated case. I've seen it in many people I've encountered.

Do not let it happen to you.

That is the stage in your life when you wish you had more time to fulfil your desires.

If you believe in the Karma philosophy, you will get another chance to fulfil them in a new life. However, YOU must start again at the beginning, in a woman's womb.

In that case, is it your death or a new life with full potential and possibilities? According to Karma, *Jananam sukhadam, Maranam karunam* in Sanskrit, birth is joyous and death is compassion.

If you don't understand yourself, make conscious decisions, and choose happiness, it is very likely that you will find yourself in the same situation in your new life as well—and the cycle will repeat.

Adi Shankaracharya, a great Indian spiritual scholar, summed it up more than a thousand years ago in just three lines as follows:

Punarapi jananam, Punarapi maranam
Punarapi janani jathare shayanam
Iha samsare bahudustare—krpaya pare Pahi Murare

In Sanskrit, it means:

Being born again, dying again
Lying again in the mother's womb
This cycle of life is so hard to cross—please help me find liberation

Dying Early

We all have two lives. The second one begins when we realise we only have one. Once you internalise this reality, you'll spend your time only on what is truly important to you.

You know that all the people you see today will die one day. Those who died yesterday had plans for this morning. We don't know how long we will live. Death can show up at any time, like an actor coming on stage with no concept of timing, and in the blink of an eye, everything can change.

A cardiac arrest, an accident, an earthquake, a tsunami, a hurricane, lightning, or even the sting of a small venomous insect can spoil the game. All that you have, including yourself, could vanish in no time.

Even though you are standing at a place where more people have died than are now living, you may not think it can happen to you. This is natural because that is how all human beings think. This is hope, which enables us to plan for the future, even though there is no guarantee you will get a sound sleep tonight and wake up tomorrow.

The lives of those who have faced death through life-threatening situations, chronic illness, or trauma have undergone significant transformations, acquiring greater mental strength, compassion, tolerance, and fulfillment.

Many individuals who have faced terminal illness express that they began to live life more fully, as their inhibitions and fear of failure had already faded. While I wouldn't wish these experiences on you in reality, I believe simulating them could offer valuable insights.

Here's how you could simulate the experience:

Before going to sleep, take a slow, gentle approach to set aside everything you have gained in life. This includes your body, physical appearance, nationality, ethnicity, religion, level of education, ideas, possessions, social status, relationships, and everything else you're attached to. Imagine yourself on your deathbed with just two to three minutes to live and your loved ones standing beside you, gazing at you.

Visualise sleep as akin to your final moments, when you may not wake up again. As you know, millions do not wake up from their sleep each day, and one day, you too will experience the same. If you fail to inhale after an exhalation, that breath could be your last, and you will cease to exist.

Remember, if you're not here from tomorrow onwards, nothing will stop anything or anyone beyond a temporary disruption. While grappling with this reality may evoke a bit of struggle and fear, with time, you'll come to internalise and accept it.

You will experience sound sleep, and upon waking up, it will feel like a new birth or fresh beginning. You may even pinch yourself to confirm your reality. Being alive and having more time to utilise what you have and pursue your desires will fill you with gratitude and happiness. As a result, you'll become more mindful and focused on what truly matters to you.

Of course, detaching from what you hold most dear is the greatest challenge here

Lord Ganesha is among the most revered deities in India, and is believed to remove obstacles from one's path to progress in life. The annual Ganesha festival is widely celebrated, with devotees flocking to markets to purchase new Ganesha idols of their choice.

These idols depict Ganesha performing various activities, such as playing football, holding a cricket bat, playing musical instruments, reading a book, relaxing, and so on. This diverse representation reflects the practice of choosing and worshipping the form of God that inspires each individual, known in Sanskrit as *Ishta Devata*.

During the ten-day festival, devotees worship the Ganesha idol with deep reverence. They adorn the idol with flowers and garlands, light lamps, prepare his favourite foods as offerings, sing and dance in celebration, and engage in various rituals. As the days progress, their affection for the idol grows, becoming a source of happiness and joy for them.

On the tenth day, it is customary to immerse the Ganesha idol in water, where it gradually dissolves. This moment is often accompanied by tears, especially from children, as they bid farewell to the idol they had worshipped and loved dearly. Amid the celebrations and joy, the pain of parting also emerges, yet this act teaches them the valuable lesson of letting go of something they hold dear.

Every festival around the world carries the meaning and purpose of helping people grasp and embrace the reality, simplicity, and beauty of life—when celebrated with reverence and mindfulness, of course.

Don't dismiss tradition outright. While some traditions may be solutions to problems that no longer exist, many of them contain wisdom accumulated over generations, evolving in ways beyond our limited capacity to comprehend.

Though they may seem rigid, they continue to evolve, with much remaining unchanged during our brief time on Earth. Observe, learn from, and internalise them, while also questioning and reshaping them to suit current contexts and needs, making them more inclusive and beneficial for all, including future generations.

Let's explore the practice of *Bhiksha*, a Sanskrit term meaning begging for alms. It differs from begging for sustenance; instead, it serves as a powerful process for self-realisation, often undertaken during pilgrimages and in spiritual contexts.

Anyone can undertake this practice. Here's how it works:

Don't use any form of transportation, not even a bicycle, to seek *Bhiksha*. Go alone and walk. Carry a bowl and accept whatever you receive in this bowl. Bring a simple cloth bag to carry the offerings you collect from multiple people. Keep your appearance simple and speak only when absolutely necessary. Approach people with a bowed head and silently extend your bowl to ask for *Bhiksha*. Avoid smiling or using any other gestures.

Take *Bhiksha* from at least twenty-one people; ideally from forty, or even more. You may need to approach many more people over several days to reach these numbers, as some may not acknowledge you or offer anything. Accept all that is given to you with sincere gratitude and without preference or aversion. Donate the food after taking what you need.

After you have collected all the money and valuables through patience and hard work, donate them to a place of worship or charity. Throughout this process, many assumptions, prejudices, pride, inhibitions, embarrassment, and fear of failure will fade away, revealing your true self and what truly matters to you.

It will help you realise and internalise the futility of accumulating unnecessary possessions, ultimately leaving everything behind for someone, somewhere, someday.

As Lord Krishna states in the Bhagavad Gita, 'Whatever you have taken is only from here, whatever you have given is only from here; whatever is yours today will belong to someone else tomorrow, and on another day, it will belong to yet another.'

This encapsulates the reality and beauty of life, along with the simplicity of death.

Death and Beyond

What happens after death? Why are after-death rituals so elaborate? Do ghosts exist? What should one watch out for? There are many questions, aren't there?

According to science, after death, your body, your mind, and YOU are all gone; it is all over.

However, according to Karma philosophy, your death is a different dimension of your life. Let us explore both, as we have done with your birth.

Science

I trust you recall our earlier conversation about how your mind works. We discussed how sensory perceptions and thoughts are decoded by your neural network, generating reactions in your body. The combinations of these perceptions and thoughts stored within you determine how you relate to and respond to others.

When a person dies, there won't be new inputs from them, which is quite obvious. Even your thoughts and feelings about that person will change once they are no longer alive. This is because they were associated with their body and mind, which no longer exist. You must make corresponding changes in your neural network about that person to ensure appropriate reactions in the changed context.

Your mind and your reactions to the deceased begin to adapt more quickly to reality through after-death rituals. These rituals help form new neural pathways and dissolve old ones—much like updating the software on a device.

If this process does not occur, those who were closely connected to the deceased may experience erratic thoughts or behaviours related to them, often referred to as being 'under the influence of a ghost.' If left unaddressed, this can lead to psychological disturbances or even serious mental health issues.

This is why after-death rituals are often elaborate and significant across most cultures and religions as they help the living transition and heal.

Karma

According to Karma philosophy, at death, you lose your body, mind, names and thoughts, but not YOU, if your desires remain unfulfilled. Moreover, YOU will get another chance to fulfil them in a subsequent life. However, if all desires are satisfied, there is no need for another life, and you attain *Moksha*, liberation from the cycle of birth and death, which is considered the ultimate goal of life in Karma philosophy.

If you had unfulfilled desires at the time of your death, your life energy or YOU will be waiting to enter a new body to begin its new life. Your life energy will be much more compulsive if you have many unfulfilled desires, and hence the next life will also start with a similar level of compulsion.

Conversely, if you have fulfilled most of your desires, you will have grown more content, composed, and happy and your life energy will be less compulsive. However, if you still require another life to satisfy any remaining desires, the next life will be significantly less compulsive unless you develop additional desires during your new lifetime.

That is your baseline level of happiness, as discussed in the happiness formula, largely determined by your karmic memory. You will soon return to that level of happiness regardless of whether good or bad events occur.

If your life energy is awaiting entry into a new body to fulfil desires, it should be diverted away from susceptible individuals who might inadvertently accept it, as well as other energy bodies drawing them. The rightful destination for such life energy is the new foetus, which is ready to begin its life.

It would be like having two life energies in one body if any other body were to accept it, similar to installing two different software versions on the same computer, which can only lead to malfunction.

Such individuals may exhibit split personalities, commonly referred to as being 'possessed by ghosts'.

You've likely heard stories such as the teenager describing places he's never visited, the girl who hasn't studied Sanskrit reciting verses in that language, or the daughter behaving like her father, among others.

Closer relatives of the deceased are more vulnerable to such phenomena, as they may be more deeply connected to the departed. Additionally, individuals who are mentally unwell, teenagers, and the living foetus inside the pregnant woman are considered more susceptible. Due to this, visiting the departed or the place of death is restricted for such individuals.

According to Karma philosophy, after-death rituals are important for the deceased to direct their life energy towards a suitable new body to fulfil their desires rather than clinging to the existing ones.

For those close to the deceased, these rituals help prevent unintentionally harbouring the life energy of the departed and facing difficulties. Moreover, they facilitate changes in their neural network to align with the new reality.

That is why, if the body of the deceased is not found, an effigy made of grass is created, and the rituals are carried out. Similarly, if someone could not attend the death rituals due to unavoidable reasons, they may perform them later in the presence of a photograph or an item that belonged to the deceased.

It is advisable for those who were close to the deceased to participate in these rituals, as it aids in updating their life software accordingly. Additionally, it allows them to fully express emotions that may be difficult to express elsewhere, whether through quiet contemplation, discussing memories of the deceased, loud crying or prolonged weeping. These emotional releases facilitate faster adaptation to the new reality. It is important not to suppress emotions or interfere with others' expressions during such occasions.

It is not advisable for those close to the deceased to touch others, share food, or take part in religious, auspicious, or social activities until the life energy of the departed has settled. Less compulsive life energies typically take eleven to fourteen days to settle, while more compulsive ones may take up to forty-one to forty-eight days. These durations hold significance in after-death rituals.

Additionally, every year, a shorter and simpler version of the rituals is performed, known as the feast to the departed—which also serves as an opportunity for family gatherings. It is worth remembering that the deceased would have cherished such gatherings with loved ones when they were alive.

As you may recall, crows can detect different types of energy in their surroundings. During after-death rituals, the behaviour of crows, particularly their willingness to approach people and consume the food offerings, serves as an indication of how far the energies of the deceased person have settled and moved on.

Always prioritise taking care of your body and mind, as they are your only resources for pursuing your life's goals. Avoid anything that weakens them. That's one of the reasons we discussed death in such detail.

Focus on being happy and joyful while you are alive, rather than worrying about what comes after death. Live with exuberance and grace, and sign off in style when it's time to say goodbye!

Celebrate Your Life

Life is not a problem to solve, but an opportunity to explore. Discover yourself, prioritise what truly matters, love what you do, and celebrate your life!

We have explored every aspect of your life—from birth to death, and everything in between: your possibilities, your responsibilities, and your potential to do your best, to succeed, and to be happy and joyful.

When you're not feeling good, it becomes difficult to do anything good. This, in turn, can reduce your happiness even further. Breaking free from this cycle is essential to rediscovering happiness and joy.

Understanding yourself, along with a sound mind and a healthy body, is essential for achieving this. As you become a better person, everything around you will also change for the better. Your knowledge, skills, wealth, and relationships can all contribute to your success—so long as you are not standing in your own way.

Success demands consistent effort. It involves gaining a solid education, developing your skills, staying physically active, maintaining a nutritious diet, training your mind, excelling at work, building positive relationships, contributing to the world around you, and more. It does not arise from merely reading, thinking, or analysing—but through understanding and consistent practice.

How many people are willing to put in that kind of effort—not for anything else, but for their own success?

Only about 10 percent.

And it's no coincidence that a similar percentage truly understand what matters most to them.

Be one of them—not part of the 90 percent majority—if you want to succeed, be happy, and celebrate your life.

Many people say it's too late to change, but the truth is, you can start changing everything from now on. Perhaps the best time was years ago, but now is your next best chance. It doesn't matter who you were before or who you are today, but what you can be tomorrow.

At thirty, you're only just beginning your life after a period of intense learning and skill development. At forty-five, half your life still lies ahead. Even at sixty, one-third of your life still lies ahead. Your life is much longer than you think.

Age is merely a number and doesn't define who you are or what you have. What truly matters at any stage of life is how well your needs and desires are fulfilled, and your physical and mental fitness to pursue them. Age becomes a hindrance only if you allow it.

The book you're reading now, the tools you use, the seeds you plant, the path you run, the bicycle you ride, the stage you perform on, and even many people around you don't know your age. If you were unaware of your age, how old would you be? You only need to stop holding yourself back.

Every change is difficult at the start and confusing in the middle, but it will lead to greatness in the end. It pushes you out of your comfort zone, often leaving you confused, vulnerable, or afraid. It may cause tension, misunderstanding, or even alienation in your relationships. But as you embrace change, a new circle of—those who genuinely resonate with your values will enter your life.

What you lose is only what was built for a person you no longer are and perhaps never wanted to be. Ensure you are kind to the past versions of yourself that were unaware of the things you know now.

Today is the first day of the rest of your life. There is no better day to begin than today. Start now—not tomorrow or someday. Do not wait for the perfect circumstances, as they may never arrive.

If you don't take a step forward and move ahead, you will always remain where you are. The gap always exists between the potential for making something possible and the lack of effort to make it happen.

When you wake up tomorrow morning, you have two choices: go back to sleep and continue dreaming, or get up and pursue your dream.

Take pride in how far you have come and have faith in how far you can go. Everything you touch on this planet carries a proud legacy—make sure you add to it.

Your life is your message—make it an inspiring one.

By internalising the concepts and practicing the techniques we discussed, you can transform your life forever. This will make the seven steps easier for you, bringing happiness and joy like you may never have experienced before.

How do you know if you are progressing well with each step?

How can you be sure you're truly experiencing happiness and joy—not merely pretending?

Checking your progress against expected outcomes provides a reliable measure to gauge your development and encourage improvement.

1. Understanding yourself, knowing what is best for you, and engaging fully with those activities are crucial for your success and happiness. Discover yourself and make conscious choices to prioritise what matters to you and what brings you joy.

    Check: clarity of thought, focused mind, minimal distractions, loving what you do, time flying.

2. Everything in life happens twice—first in your mind, then in reality. Train your mind to choose one thought over another, reshape your beliefs, maintain a positive mindset, and explore new possibilities.

    Check: no doubts or confusion, clear communication, feeling in control.

3. To fulfil your needs and desires, you rely on your physical body. Take great care of it to ensure smooth and efficient functioning. Regular physical exercise, a healthy diet, adequate sleep, and self-care are essential.

    Check: Well-prepared, fewer mistakes, energetic throughout the day, more productive.

4. Maintaining positive relationships with everyone and everything around you is vital to your success and happiness. Diligently build, strengthen, and nurture meaningful relationships based on mutual support and sharing.

Check: fewer complaints about anything or anyone, more positivity, rarely angry.

5. Right is right even if no one is doing it. Wrong is wrong even if everyone is doing it. Always uphold righteousness by being responsible towards yourself, your family, society, and the environment.

    Check: not worried about the past, not scared of the future, low anxiety, less fear.

6. Any work you do aims to fulfil your needs or desires and contribute to the betterment of others' lives. Prioritise learning and skill development, and collaborate with anyone or anything to perform your tasks with the utmost quality and efficiency.

    Check: not bored, not exhausted, not stuck, creative, know how to proceed.

7. Everything you possess today comes from here, and you are not the sole cause of your success. Be grateful to everyone and everything that has shaped who you are and what you have, and give back for all that you have received—and continue to receive.

    Check: gratitude, humility, high self-esteem, compassion, contentment.

It will work for you, regardless of your age, gender, wealth, social standing, level of education, place of residence, or personal circumstances. In fact, it will work for everyone willing to learn, unlearn, and change.

There are no new concepts or theories here. Nothing mysterious or abstract. It is all encoded within you, like a user manual for your life. It's the same for me as well, except for what's truly important to you. Perhaps you weren't paying close enough attention to notice.

It does not matter. You have everything now. You're ready to go on your own from here.

It has been my privilege to walk alongside you and speak with you, holding your hand throughout this journey. You wouldn't have stayed with me this long unless you had already chosen to be successful, happy, and joyful.

I have no doubt you will enjoy the rest of your journey, live a life you are truly proud of, and help others do the same. I hope to see you there soon.

That is my heartfelt wish and blessing for you.

Made in the USA
Monee, IL
03 May 2026